Luleå
of Bothnia
Finland
Åbo
HELSINGFORS
Leningrad
Åland
Tallin
M
Estonia
Latvia
Riga
Lithuania

A CONCISE HISTORY OF SWEDEN

Alf Åberg

A concise HISTORY of SWEDEN

Translated by
Gordon Elliott, M. A. (St And.)

Natur och Kultur

First edition published by LTs förlag 1985
in cooperation with The Swedish Museums
Association and The Board of Museum Directors
in Stockholm

Translated from the Swedish edition 1985:
Sveriges historia i fickformat

Cover design Anders Rahm
Front cover: The Hunninge stone, eight century,
Buttle, Gotland (photo Carl O Löfman) and
Gustavus III in royal attire, drawing by
Johan Tobias Sergel, c. 1785.
Back cover: The crown of Eric XIV, 1561
(photo The Royal Treasury, Stockholm).

Bokförlaget Natur och Kultur, Stockholm
Art editor Lena Nordström
Map Sven-Arne Åkerling
Fourth edition
Printed by Kristianstads Boktryckeri AB 1994
ISBN 91-27-04021-6

Contents

The Swedish Royal Family: King Charles XVI Gustavus and Queen Silvia with their children. From the left: Prince Charles Philip, Princess Madeleine and Crown Princess Victoria. Photo by Charles Hammarsten, Allers Photo Press, Stockholm.

The Prehistoric Age

There was a time when the whole of Sweden was covered with ice. About 12000 BC the great icefields began to loosen their grip in the extreme south of the country. It is possible to establish the date because the ice beneath the annual thaw deposited a layer of clay above the earlier strata. Geologists have studied these different annual layers of clay and have thus worked out a reliable table for thousands of years.

Arctic plants and animals advanced into the ice-free regions and in their trail came the first human beings, tribes of nomadic hunters, who made their way from Denmark via a landbridge to Scania. Together with their hounds they hunted the reindeer, and their weapons consisted of spears and arrows. On the west coast there were fishing tribes who killed seals with their clubs and caught fish with hooks and nets.

As the ice withdrew the climate became warmer. Birch and pine trees made their appearance and formed forests. In the place of the reindeer came the animals of the forest: elk, roe deer, stag, bear and the wild boar. The number of hunters increased. A new implement was invented – an axe of flint to enable the hunter to hack his way through the forest. At Bäckaskog in Scania the skeleton of a woman has been found, the mother of several children, who belonged to the hunting folk and lived 7000–8000 years ago. She was less than five feet tall and of slender build.

It was at this time that the contours of "the earliest Sweden" began to take shape. Scania was separated from Denmark. The ice cap retreated from the wilds of Norrland, hunters and fishermen began to penetrate these regions. The hunting people did not remain long in the same place, but to judge from the finds special sites were associated with their cults. At Namforsen in the River Ångerman in Northern Sweden 1,400 carvings of figures have been found on the river banks and on the islands in the river. Most of the figures represent elks. The hunters must have believed that they could conjure forth their quarry by depicting it near the localities where the hunting was to take place.

About 5000 years ago agriculture was introduced into Sweden and a great change came about in the lives of the inhabitants. For the hunter and his family, life was a desperate struggle for sustenance. Now Man could make a permanent home in one place, live on the crops he cultivated and on the tame cattle he tended. On the Bog of Dag near Alvastra in Östergötland the remains have been found of a small community which existed 4000 years ago. The inhabitants had chosen the site on the bog as it offered protection against enemies. The community cultivated grain by the banks of the marsh, but its members also included hunters and fishermen.

The agriculturists introduced a new religion. For their dead they constructed large dolmens of stone. The dead were provided with useful objects, in addition to food and drink, which were deposited in the graves. This religion with its large stone graves was introduced from Western Europe. Possibly it was spread by immigrants or by merchants from across the seas. Gradually still larger tombs – passage graves – were constructed to provide room for several bodies.

About 2000 BC a new race, the so-called Battle Axe folk, appear to have immigrated to Sweden and to have conquered the country. It appears highly probable that these people came from the East, and they are generally assumed to have been of Indo-European stock. Possibly these were the immigrants who brought horses with them. Since that time Sweden has never fallen into the hands of foreign conquerors. After some centuries shrouded in mystery a new type of communal grave began to be constructed. These consisted of long narrow chambers, stone cists, and reveal that the population had now spread to all parts of Southern Sweden.

In the remarkable stone cist at Kivik eight high stone slabs form the long sides of the cist. The carvings show figures walking in processions and offering up sacrifices. The symbols are doubled: we see two sun discs, two horses, two axes and a two-wheeled cheriot and charioteer. Photograph: Hans Wåhlin, ATA.

About 1500 BC objects of bronze began to be manufactured, in addition to articles of flint and wood. Gold, too, began to play an increasingly important part. A new age had dawned – the Bronze Age. Skillful smiths created articles of rare beauty and richness of design. The men carried axes, spears and swords, and the women wore ornaments, pins of bronze, necklaces and belt plates in ornately decorated spiral patterns.

All metals had to be imported and only chiefs could afford to buy them. The Bronze Age was the age of magnates. The large communal graves disappeared and were replaced by huge mounds of stones and earth, providing a resting place for only a few persons of distinction. The Bronze Age was a period of extensive communications throughout Europe, and cultural influence followed the trade routes. The religious conceptions of the people of the Bronze Age had their origins in Greece and Crete. The rock-carvings in the impressive tombs at Kivik in Scania bear witness to elaborate funerary rites. In the case of other rock-carvings, especially those in the parish of Tanum in Bohuslän, we find a pictorial saga involving ships, ploughs, axes and spears, all of them seemingly a greeting to the sun and fertility.

Another revolution in human life occurred about 500 BC, when iron was first extracted from the bog ore formed at the bottom of the lakes. Iron became a useful metal, a common property as it was obtainable in Sweden, and was therefore inexpensive. At the beginning of the Iron Age the climate was cold and damp. The people learned to build better houses and to wear warmer clothes. About the beginning of the Christian era the climate once more became milder.

To judge from the finds, there was extensive trade with the Roman Empire. About 100 AD the Romans first learned of the northern lands. In his book Germania, Tacitus described the nation of the Suiones, a people rich in warriors, arms and fleets. The Suiones have always been identified with the Svea, the people inhabiting the shores and islands of Lake Mälaren in Central Sweden. About 500 AD Uppland became

The 2.5 metre tall rune stone at Möjebro,in the heart of the Svea Kingdom north-west of Uppsala, was erected to the memory of Frarad. Photograph: ATA.

the new leading settlement in the country. At Gamla Uppsala and Vendel mighty burial mounds were raised over the local kings, while others were interred in their ships. Some of these early kings – Ottar and Adils – are named in the Old English epic poem *The Song of Beowulf.* They are also referred to in the Old Icelandic poem *Ynglingatal.*

The land continued to rise from the waters. New soil could be subjected to the plough, and the population spread to the coastal plain of Norrland and to the inland regions in the north of Uppland. The farmers formed village communities which cooperated with each other. The names of many of these Iron Age villages have survived and tell us how the land was first put to use. Hundreds of ancient forts bear witness to times of war. At Eketorp on Öland a small circular fort, with a diameter of about 80 yards, has been restored. There the inhabitants lived in houses built together radially from the inside of the wall.

The oldest picture stones on Gotland date from the Fifth and Sixth Centuries. They display figures of human beings, beasts and vessels associated with long-forgotten sagas of heroes and gods. From this time rune stones begin to tell us about individual people. The most remarkable is the rune stone at Rök in Östergötland with its lengthy and difficult message concerned with ancient heroic poems and legends.

There were still no towns in the lands of the Svea. On the other hand the remains of a large trading centre have been found on the island of Helgö in Lake Mälaren. Craftsmen had a settlement there and produced various articles – glass, ceramics, locks and other metal objects.

The farming community was consolidated, internal colonization continued, trade increased and was extended within and beyond Sweden. This was the background to the voyages of the Vikings.

The Viking Age

It was about the year 800 that the long and bold viking voyages east and west over sea began. These expeditions were at the same time both warlike and commercial. Even in earlier times the people of the Nordic lands had traded with their neighbours. Now they embarked on still longer journeys, and it was the internal weaknesses of the states to the east and west which permitted the Scandinavian expansion. The primary condition for these voyages was the flat-bottomed viking ship, whether under sail or propelled by oars. The vessels could be beached anywhere along the shallow coastal shores or could make their way up the wide sluggish rivers. Scania, Blekinge, Halland and Bohuslän belonged to Denmark, and the men from these regions followed the Danes and Norwegians on viking expeditions westwards to the British Isles and Western France as well as to the large islands in the Atlantic, Iceland and Greenland. The rune stones tell us that many Swedish vikings took part in the expeditions to the west. A large proportion of them were peaceful merchants and farmers who settled permanently in the new country.

The Svea people and the Gotlanders travelled mainly to the east. For the most part they were merchants and their voyages led them via the Russian rivers to some of the world's greatest trading centres. On one of the routes Kiev was their principal station, where the Rus folk, the Nordic merchants, gathered and whence they made their way along the River Dnieper to the Black Sea and ultimately to Constantinopel, which they called Miklagård, the Great City.

The other commercial route followed the Volga to the regions around the Caspian Sea, which the Vikings called Serk-

Several large grave-fields have been found outside the walls of Birka. This picture is of one of these, Hemlanden, which with its 1,600 graves, mainly mounds, was probably the largest in Scandinavia during the Viking Age. Photograph: Nils Lagergren, ATA.

land, the Land of Silk. Many of them made their way still further, to Baghdad, the great trading metropolis of the Arab world.

The sword was the basic weapon of the Vikings. But they were also equipped with helmets, shields and battle axes with long helves. Two of their principal commodities were furs and prisoners, whom they seized on the way and later sold as slaves.

Many Vikings brought home articles of great value from successful expeditions: reliquaries, church plate, objects of glass and yokes of bronze. They also gave ornaments to their wives who had stayed at home. With them they brought many silver coins from the Arab world and the lands of Western Europe. Coins of this kind have been discovered in many places and especially on Gotland. The Vikings also acquired a knowledge of weapons and of the science of fortifications. They also brought back a knowledge of Christianity, which was to change the pattern of their lives and link their countries more closely to the rest of Europe.

During the Viking Age the first trading city was founded in the Svea land. It was called Birka and was located on an island in Lake Mälaren. The permanent population was between 1,000 and 2,000 people. The expansion of trade with foreign parts stimulated the growth of the town. The laws of the Svea King were observed. He guaranteed peace at the

At Birka, the earliest commercial town in the Svea land, there was a Christian mission. Among numerous finds made there is this silver crucifix from about 900. It is now preserved at the Museum of National Antiquities. Photograph: Sören Hallgren, Mus. Nat. Ant.

market and gave his protection to the foreign traders. In the town the men were clad in knee-length coats and trousers, with a belt around the waist and over all a cloak. The women wore a skirt and a shawl. Their dresses were adorned with trinkets and jewellery, and from their waists hung a bunch of scissors, knives, pins, keys and other valuables.

About 830 Ansgar, the first Christian apostle in Scandinavia, arrived at Birka. The Svea people still believed in a clan of gods, the Asa; their most important gods were Odin, Thor and Frey, who were praised at great sacrificial feasts at Gamla Uppsala. Ansgar was granted permission to preach at

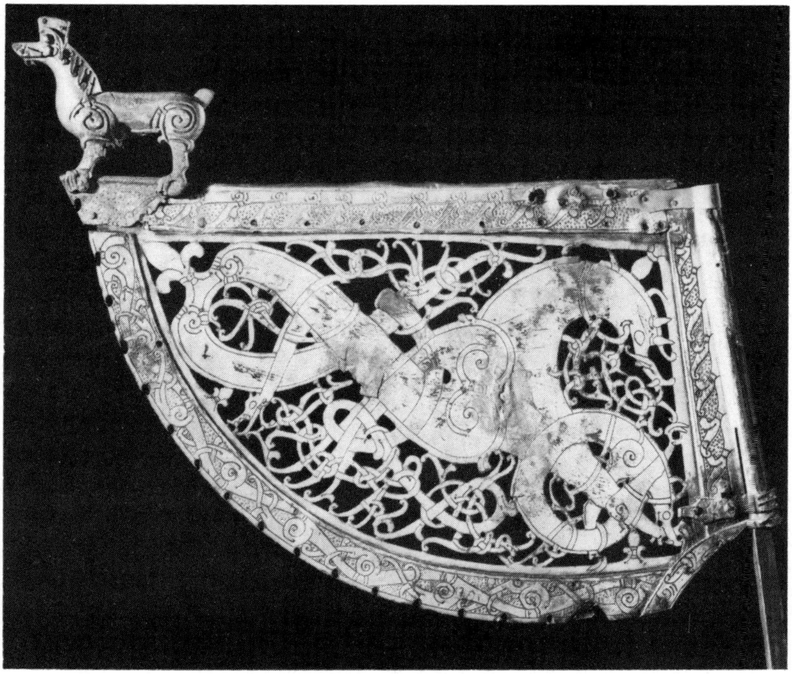

In Söderala Church, Hälsingland, is preserved this magnificent weather-vane once a standard at the mast-head or on the stem of a warship in the Eleventh Century. It may be seen at the Museum of National Antiquities. Photograph: Sören Hallgren, Mus. Nat. Ant.

Birka. He was mainly active among the Christian thralls who had been taken prisoner abroad, but he also won some of the Svea folk to his faith.

After Ansgar other Christian missionaries continued his work, but several hundred years elapsed before the Christian faith triumphed. We can follow the work of the missions with the help of the rune stones raised over many Christians. "May God and the Mother of God succour his soul and his spirit" is inscribed on a stone bearing the Christian cross.

The Viking Age lasted until the mid-Eleventh Century. Several rune stones describe the last major expedition to the Russian regions. This was commanded by the viking chieftain Ingvar the Far-Travelled, and many ships with men from different provinces took part in the campaign. This seems to have ended in a disaster and many, perhaps all, the men perished. A rune stone at Gripsholm Castle describes the fate of some of Ingvar's followers: "In manly mood they sought gold afar and gave eagles food in eastern lands. They died in the south in Serkland."

During the Viking Age the Kingdoms of Denmark and Sweden took shape, but the border between them consisted of large uninhabited wildernesses in the west and south. Water linked the various parts together. A sea voyage took much less time than travelling overland.

The Swedish Kingdom was a federation of provinces independent of each other. All they had in common was the King and the sacrificial festivals at the heathen temple at Gamla Uppsala. There was no council of the realm and the powers of the King were as yet limited.

Every province had its own laws and its *Thing* or assembly. The large tribes or clans in the provinces to the south of the Svea lands were known as the Goths. Västergötland is the earliest of the old Swedish provinces, and it is likely that Östergötland was colonized from that province. Fierce battles for the crown were fought between powerful families in Västergötland and Uppland. South of both Gothic provinces lay the small lands bordering on the Danish kingdom.

The Founding of the Kingdom

The efforts of the missionaries resulted in the victory of the Christian faith, and although the ancient Asa religion put up considerable resistance, the Church was soon able to organize itself. Birka, Sweden's oldest town, had been abandoned as early as the end of the Eleventh Century, but new urban communities had been founded. By the beginning of the Twelfth Century provincial sees had been established at Skara, Linköping, Eskilstuna, Strängnäs, Sigtuna and Västerås.

Of the earliest cathedrals in Sweden only the ruins of one remain to be seen – St Peter's Church at Sigtuna. The King had his residence in that town, and the oldest dated coins were minted there. The buildings at Sigtuna followed the shore of Lake Mälaren and thence narrow lanes led up to the market street, where the merchants had their homes and booths. Smiths laboured in their workshops and their products were exported. The houses were small, constructed of branches and filled in with clay.

In the 1130's the episcopal see was transferred from Sigtuna to Gamla Uppsala, where a cathedral was erected on the site of the demolished heathen temple. In 1164 a Swedish archbishopric was established here. Within a short time the archbishop moved to the lively trading centre on the River Fyris, which was given the name of Uppsala. There work started on the building of a new cathedral.

During the Twelfth Century a Christian community began to take shape. Churches were built everywhere, first of wood and then of stone. Many village names still remind us of the ancient gods – Odensvi, Torsvi and Frölunda. The churches were thought to provide protection against evil spirits. "My voice is the terror of all evil spirits" is inscribed on the old church bell at Bälinge Church in Uppland.

Every province had its laws. Originally these existed only in oral form. In the province there lived a lawman who spoke at the *Thing* and knew all the laws by heart. The laws laid down numerous rules governing life in the villages. The laws assumed written form in the Thirteenth and Fourteenth Centuries and by then had absorbed Christian elements. Their aim was to guarantee peace and justice. The laws of Västmanland declared: "The land shall be built with law and not with deeds of violence."

Society was still dominated by the leading families. Every freeman belonged to a family, whose members were his kinsman and allies. The farm should be handed down within the immediate circle of relatives, and if it had to be sold, it should be offered first to the closest kinsfolk. The family expected much of its individual members. The manslaughter of a kinsman had to be avenged if the perpetrator belonged to another family. People took the law into their own hands, and none could avoid his duty. The Church objected to blood feuds, and the provincial laws gave them no support, but the way to a just society was long and difficult.

The thralls – and there were many of them – possessed no rights at all. Most of them were house thralls or agricultural labourers while the female thralls were employed on domestic tasks. Thralls belonged to no family and their owners possessed unrestricted rights over them. Thralls could be inherited, given away or sold like a horse or a cow. Christianity introduced a new concept of thralldom, since the Church upheld the equality of all men in the sight of God. Requiem masses were held for the dead children of female thralls as well as for those of free women. In 1335 thralldom was abolished by a royal decree issued "to the Glory of God and of Our Belessed Lady".

At about the same time blood feuds were forbidden. The dissolution of the family community and the abolition of thralldom were associated with the formation of a new kind of social order, dominated by a central Kingdom supported by the Church.

Sweden was an elective monarchy. The King was elected first by the Svea *Thing* in Uppland, and thereafter he set off on a tour so that his election could be confirmed by the assemblies of all the other provinces. Every province was still so independent at this time that the King had to request safe conduct and provide hostages at the provincial borders. Following the royal tour, the King was crowned by the Archbishop in Uppsala Cathedral. The King was entitled to the yield of the royal lands in various parts of the country. He also had the right to impose taxes and fines as well as to reward those who served him. Among the royal duties was the command of the fleet, the numerous ships with men and arms which, according to ancient tradition, were maintained in the eastern provinces.

With the aid of the fleet the King endeavoured to extend the national borders to the east. The Church supported his plans, and viking expeditions were transformed into Christian crusades against the Finns and the Estonians. St Eric, the national saint, is traditionally said to have commanded the first crusade against Finland. Birger Jarl, a leading member of the Folkunga dynasty, commanded another expedition of conquest, nominally a crusade, to Tavastland in the mid-Thirteenth Century, and by the end of the century the whole of Finland had been incorporated in the Swedish realm and its population converted to Christianity. Åbo became the seat of the new power and a centre of trade. Here, too, the earliest cathedral for the Bishop of Finland was erected.

The King and the magnates cooperated with each other during these naval operations. At the end of the Thirteenth Century the leading men of the realm were reorganized at a meeting at Alsnöhus by Lake Mälaren. The King's servants and those who served other great men of the realm with horses and weapons were promised great privileges, above all exemption from taxes. In this way a lay nobility was formed,

During the summer of 1936 the skeleton of a man, dating from the mid-Fourteenth Century, was discovered in a peat bog at Bocksten near Varberg. The man, who was in his thirties, had been murdered. In order to prevent the corpse from rising again three stakes were driven through the body. His clothing was well preserved and is now preserved at the Varberg Museum in the Fortress.

Drotten Church was situated in the centre of Old Visby and according to one view it was the oldest parish church. The church, which was consecrated to the Lord Himself, was built about 1200 and has a tower more than 105 feet high. Photograph: B. Gustafsson, ATA.

an aristocracy which was to spread throughout the entire country. The King chose his lieutenants from this class. The most important of these was the *Jarl*, Earl, who commanded the fleet in the absence of the King.

Great castles date from this time – at Nyköping and Stegeborg, Kalmar and Borgholm, Jönköping and Lödöse, Västerås and Örebro – places where the King resided on his tours through the country. Royal sheriffs were quartered in the castles, and the peasants paid their taxes to these officials. The castles signified that Sweden had now become a kingdom. About 1350 King Magnus Eriksson abolished the old provincial laws in favour of laws which applied to the entire realm.

Agriculture and animal husbandry were the main sources of livelihood. The peasants lived in villages where the culti-

The walls of Visby are the largest and best preserved mediaeval structure in Sweden. This picture shows a section of the East Wall near the Dalman Gate. Work started on the wall in the mid-Thirteenth Century and it was reinforced with hanging turrets about 1300, thus enabling the defenders to shoot along the wall. Photograph: Raymond Hejdström, Gotlands fornsal.

vated soil was apportioned in allotments according to the location of the farms in the village. The land was cultivated communally. Grain was the prevalent crop and was used to make bread, porridge and ale. In the forested districts stock-farming was most common. The domestic animals raised under starvation conditions during the winter were very small. Strict laws governed domestic life in the villages. Under the protection of the Church and the growing power of the state the peasants learned to pay hitherto unknown taxes.

In the Thirteenth Century the burghers made their appearance. The Hanseatic towns of Northern Germany had taken over the Baltic trade, and lively commercial contacts led to the growth of many new towns, mainly on the Baltic coast and the shores of Lake Mälaren. They were often surrounded by walls and dominated by German merchants.

The new inland towns – Västerås, Arboga, Köping and

St Birgitta at her writing desk. Wooden sculpture in a triptych, Törnevalla Church, Östergötland, late Fifteenth Century. Now at the Museum of National Antiquities. Photograph: Marianne Gustafsson, Mus. Nat. Ant.

Örebro – were indebted to mining for their growing prosperity. The Falun copper mine was being rationally exploited in the Thirteenth Century. One century later state-controlled mining was taking place in the Bergslagen region with royal sheriffs and tax-paying miners who, together with their workers, extracted the ore from the mines.

Where Lake Mälaren flows into the salt waters a castle was built for defence against pirates. Birger Jarl determined that a town should be built on the island where the castle was located. The town was named Stockholm, and it attracted merchants and craftsmen. In time it became the capital of Sweden.

During the Thirteenth Century Gotland enjoyed a golden age. Many churches and commercial buildings were erected on the island. Visby was a centre of the North German merchants' trade and it became one of the largest and richest cities of the entire Baltic region. The city was surrounded by a strong circular wall, large parts of which have been preserved. The ruins of stately churches and numerous mediaeval commercial buildings still remind us of Visby's distinguished past.

During the period when the realm was being founded the Church exercised great privileges. It had its own courts and taxation system, and when the religious orders came to Sweden the King supported the monasteries with generous gifts. Among the oldest were Alvastra and Varnhem in Östergötland, Nydala in Småland and Roma on Gotland. The most remarkable of all was Vadstena in Östergötland, home of the Order of St Birgitta, the creation of St Birgitta herself, and the spiritual centre of Sweden in late mediaeval times.

The Union of Kalmar

In 1397 councillors, noblemen and prelates from the Nordic countries assembled for a meeting at Kalmar Castle. They had been summoned by the Danish-Norwegian Queen Margaret, who had now become the ruler of Sweden. Her great vision was to being about a permanent union of the northern lands under a common monarchy. At Kalmar her youthful kinsman Eric of Pomerania was crowned King of the three realms. Agreement was reached that peace should always be maintained between the kingdoms and that they would never be separated from each other.

Queen Margaret died in 1412, and already in the reign of her successor the union was threatened. Eric of Pomerania sought to increase the royal power and wished to merge the three kingdoms into a single absolute monarchy. He embittered the Swedish nobles by appointing Germans and Danes as bailiffs in Swedish castles. Eric desired to break the Hanseatic trade monopoly in the Baltic region and became involved in a lengthy war with the North German cities. This compelled him to impose taxes on the Swedes and to demand their military assistance.

Widespread dissatisfaction with the King resulted in 1434 in a peasant rising in Sweden led by Engelbrekt, member of a wealthy mining family. The nobles and the Church made common cause with Engelbrekt, and after Engelbrekt's death two years later a nobleman, Karl Knutsson, was elected Regent and subsequently King of Sweden.

During the days of Engelbrekt Parliaments, *Riksdag*, were summoned to reach important decisions on behalf of the people. Apart from representatives of the nobility, the clergy and

In the Fifteenth Century, during the Union of Kalmar, Karl Knutsson was three times King of Sweden. Bernt Notke's sculpture of him is preserved in the National Portrait Collection at Gripsholm Castle. We see him kneeling at prayer supported by his shield which bears the Royal Arms of Sweden. Photograph: ATA.

the burghers, the peasantry also sent members to the Riksdag, but we cannot speak until the 1460's of a true Riksdag consisting of four Estates, each of which made independent resolutions.

On several occasions the Danish Kings of the Union recovered their power in Sweden. In a renowned battle at Brunkeberg in Stockholm the Danish King was defeated by the Swedish Regent Sten Sture. His victory was celebrated every year as a major ecclesiastical and national day of rejoicing. In commemoration a large statue of St George was raised in the Great Church of Stockholm. This became the symbol of the Swedish national state which now began to take shape.

National feeling was also reflected in the cultural sphere. In 1477 a university was founded at Uppsala – the oldest in Scandinavia. By the close of the Fifteenth Century books were being printed in Swedish at Stockholm and Uppsala. The language was still impoverished and full of loanwords from Latin, Danish and Low German, yet it had developed considerably from the days of the provincial laws.

In ecclesiastical art creativeness flourished. At Härkeberga Church in Uppland the painter Albrekt has left us pictures from the Bible inspired by daily life in Uppland. At Arentuna Church we see Adam and Eve as Uppland peasants illustrating the classless society before the Fall of Man – according to a song from the days of the peasant rebellions in England:

> "When Adam delved and Eve span,
> Who was then the gentleman?"

In 1520 King Christian II of Denmark was crowned King of Sweden. He executed about one hundred members of the independence party in a bloodbath in the Great Square of Stockholm, but he failed in his attempt to restore the Union of Kalmar by force.

The Vasa Period

At Christmas in 1520 a rising against King Christian broke out in the traditionally rebellious province of Dalecarlia. Its leader was a youthful nobleman, Gustav Eriksson Vasa. The Danish army was defeated and the independence movement grew rapidly. Councillors and bishops supported the rising, and on 6th June 1523 Gustavus Vasa was elected King of Sweden at a national assembly. Stockholm opened its gates, and on Midsummer Eve the King rode into his liberated capital. The foundations had now been laid for a national Swedish state.

Chaos prevailed throughout the realm. The King needed money to pay his army and stabilize the finances, and he knew where to find the money. At a riksdag at Västerås in 1527 he was given a free hand to confiscate Church property. At that time the Church and the monasteries owned one-fifth of all the farms in the country or as many as did the nobility. The confiscation of all these lands enriched the state.

The Late Mediaeval Church collapsed and the King became Head of the Church. One support for his actions was to be found in the Lutheran doctrines which were being preached at the time by the reformer Olaus Petri. In time the Church broke away from Rome and became the Lutheran Established Church which it still is today.

The large-scale confiscations of land gave the King and his servants the possibility of implementing extensive modernization of the administration and the levying of taxes. Throughout the realm the King built strong castles for defence and administration. At Uppsala and Vadstena the King built castles to demonstrate his power over the Church. In other

In 1520 the Union King Christian II executed some eighty followers of Sten Sture the Younger. This so-called Bloodbath of Stockholm took place in the Great Square of the Old Town. Photograph: Svante Geggen.

cases, such as Gripsholm, he rebuilt the mediaeval castles. The castles were also used for the purposes of representation. The King and his court stayed at the castles, and taxes in kind were gathered locally and consumed on the spot.

Gustavus Vasa sought absolute power and ruled Sweden in accordance with his will. To many he appeared to be a tyrant, but considered solely from the point of view of beneficial government his long reign was an unqualified success. He liberated Sweden from commercial dependence on the Hanseatic League, creating thereby the necessary conditions for an independent Swedish foreign policy. He enriched the state, established an hereditary monarchy and reorganized the national defence. For the first time the Bible was printed in Swedish, and its treasury of words became an important part of the common Swedish heritage.

During the Sixteenth Century the population of Sweden was about 800,000 and that of Finland about 200,000. Only 5 per cent of the population lived in towns. A corresponding percentage may have been engaged in mining in the Bergslagen district. The remainder lived in rural districts. Peasants and agricultural labourers formed the overwhelming majority. The King eagerly encouraged the younger generation to leave the overpopulated villages and colonize the wild regions of the north. This migration took place, both in Sweden and in Finland. At the end of the Sixteenth Century numerous Finnish peasants moved to Sweden and settled in the forest areas, particularly in Värmland. In the main the country was self-supporting.

During the Vasa Age Stockholm had a permanent population of 7,000–8,000. When the court was residing at the Palace the population could increase to between 9,000 and 10,000. One-third of the inhabitants were in the service of the crown as craftsmen, soldiers or administrators. Most of the inhabitants had moved in from the country, but here could also be found people from Finland and Åland. Great influence was exercised by the 150 German families in Stockholm, thanks to their wealth and solidarity. Scots and Netherlanders also formed important groups.

Within the walls conditions were very crowded, and many people moved out to the areas immediately to the north and south. These were the areas reserved by the authorities for occupations involving noxious odours or inflammable materials. Here, too, the burghers kept their cattle, their brew houses and their bath huts.

Following the death of Gustavus Vasa, Sweden was ruled by his sons Eric, John and Charles, in that order. Their reigns witnessed the coming of the Renaissance to Sweden. Eric turned the castles into princely palaces with ornamented ceilings and panelling, and he provided their gardens with summer houses and fountains.

Eric was a good linguist, musical and talented. With Macchiavelli as his guide, he pursued a bold and aggressive

The Inner Court of Kalmar Castle with the remarkable well. During the reign of John III the well acquired its superstructure in the Italian Renaissance style. Photo: G Sörensen. Kalmar Castle.

foreign policy. He wished to gain control of the Russian trade through the Baltic ports. Estonia surrendered to Sweden, and Eric thereby laid the foundations for a Swedish Baltic empire. But in the course of his continued efforts to take over the Russian trade he became involved in wars against Denmark, Lübeck and Poland. For seven bloody years the border areas in the south were ravaged, and when peace was signed in 1570 the Swedish treasury was empty.

Eric was deposed by his brothers and died a prisoner, probably on the orders of his brother John. John's son Sigismund became King of Poland and later of Sweden. His attempt to bring about a Swedish-Polish Union failed. He was deposed by his uncle Charles IX with the result that Sweden and Poland became bitter enemies. During the last years of Charles' reign Sweden was also at war with Russia and Denmark.

Sweden becomes a Great Power

Charles IX died in 1611 and was succeeded by his son Gustavus II Adolphus. His royal achievements were to be as remarkable and celebrated as those of Gustavus Vasa. His enormous task was to raise Sweden from its weak military position and implement the Baltic policy. On his accession he was obliged to grant considerable privileges to the nobility, whose members were promised sole rights to all higher appointments, their services being permanent and salaried. The leading figure of the nobility, Axel Oxenstierna, became Chancellor of the Realm.

The King was very different from his Chancellor. He was impulsive, had far-reaching ideas and bold plans. Yet Oxenstierna with his sober caution could often bring him back to grim reality. But they complemented each other and worked together with regard to foreign policy as well as the reorganization of the administration and the armed forces.

After considerable effort Sweden succeeded in extending her Baltic possessions as far as to the borders of Russia to the east, absorbing into the realm both Estonia and the formerly Polish province of Livonia. Swedish power in the Baltic was now firmly established. Sweden could now impose customs duties on most of the merchant vessels sailing from the Baltic to Western Europe. The Baltic customs revenues became one of the richest sources of income for the state.

While the war was being fought in the east, the internal administration was being subjected to reorganization and modernisation. The University of Uppsala was required to train public officials, and Sweden acquired its first bureaucracy with its own ésprit-de-corps and loyalty to authority.

During the reign of Gustavus II Adolphus the University of Uppsala was restored. A stately University Building, the Gustavianum, was erected in 1625 with lecture halls and accommodation for students in the upper storey. Photograph: Ultraförlaget.

Gustavus II Adolphus was just as interested as Gustavus Vasa had been in maintaing continuous contact with his subjects. He made use of the clergy, who read from the pulpits his reasons for imposing taxes and enlisting soldiers. He also exploited the prevalent hatred for the nobility by compelling them to pay new taxes. He motivated, and received support for his policy in the Riksdag where the peasants were now represented as a special estate.

The army was largely recruited from the farming community. In 1622 the infantry numbered 36,000, the cavalry 4,500 men. At the same time efforts were made to construct a number of ships of the line. This period also saw the foundation of a Swedish arms industry. Dutch merchants and Walloon smiths came to Sweden and played an important part in the development of the iron industry. The most prominent was Louis De Geer, who established an arms factory at Norrköping and several other works in Northern Uppland. Swedish troops could be armed with weapons made in Sweden.

Swedish cannons became an important export commodity, as was the copper from the Falun mine in Dalecarlia. Many new towns were founded during this period. The first and largest of these was Gothenburg at the mouth of the River Göta älv. This town, which was constructed by Dutch architects, was from the beginning a leading commercial centre. Much of the iron from the Bergslagen district was exported via Gothenburg to the Netherlands.

During the wars with Poland the King succeeded in establishing control of Danzig and other commercial ports in Prussia. In 1630 he resolved to intervene in the Thirty Years' War. The Catholic Emperor was in the process of crushing the Protestant Princes and his army was approaching the shores of the Baltic, thereby posing a threat to the growing powers of Sweden. Swedish naval vessels transported the army to Rügen. Gustavus Adolphus received the support of France, and the following year he defeated the Emperor's General Tilly at Breitenfeld.

The King's plans grew more ambitious. He wished to create an alliance between Sweden and the Protestant Princes of Germany, with himself as the principal leader. In the spring of 1632 he entered Munich, the culmination of his military fortunes. Wallenstein, the Emperor's new general, invaded Saxony and on 6th November the armies met at Lützen. The victory was won by the Swedes, but Gustavus Adolphus fell during the battle.

When Gustavus Adolphus died his only child, his daughter Christina, was only five years of age. The Council was dominated by Axel Oxenstierna who set up a Regency Government of high noblemen. Hostilities continued in Germany, the Swedish Army consisting for the most part of mercenaries

Gustavus II Adolphus' flagship Wasa *sank on her maiden voyage from Stockholm in 1628. The wreck was discovered by Anders Franzén, a research scholar, in 1956. After she had been salvaged the vessel was placed in a dock at Djurgården in Stockholm, where she was restored and became a unique tour ist attraction. The picture shows the lower gun deck of the* Wasa.

from Germany, Scotland and England. Many foreign officers took up permanent residence in Sweden and were ennobled

At the Peace of Westphalia in 1648 Sweden was granted most of Pomerania and other territorial concessions along the Baltic and North Sea coasts. Sweden was unable to acquire the Polish ports, but received instead other "splendid and valuable harbours", as Oxenstierna wrote. As a result Sweden's strategical situation had now been completely changed.

Stockholm was transformed into a representative centre for the youthful Great Power. The mediaeval city walls were razed around the Old Town and were replaced by quays and open spaces. Distinguished officials and generals, who had grown rich during the war, built magnificent residences and the aristocracy acquired a splendid place of assembly in the House of the Nobility.

During this period Sweden participated in a colonization enterprise in North America. An area along the Delaware River in the vicinity of the present town of Wilmington was purchased from the Indians. Swedes and Finns settled in the colony which received the name of New Sweden. Many of the settlers remained when the colony was conquered by the Dutch in 1655.

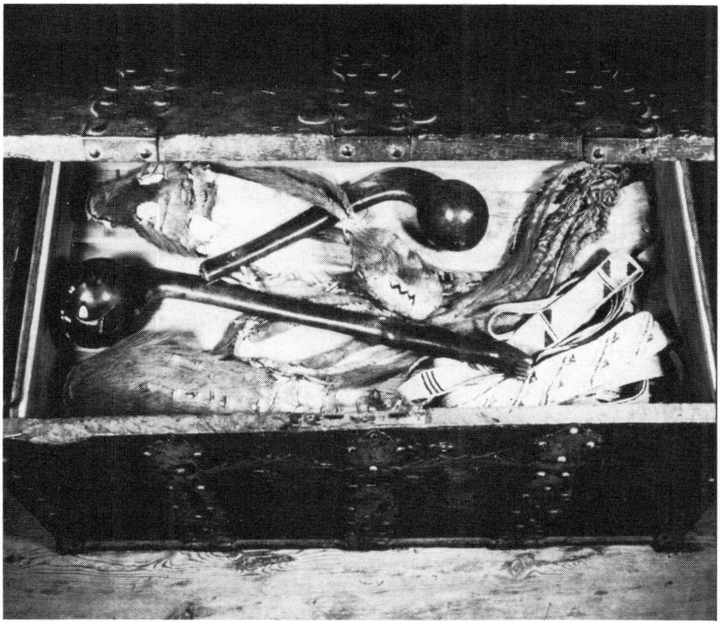

At Skokloster there is a chest containing Red Indian objects from the Swedish Colony in Delaware. These – wolf heads, slings and ceremonial clubs – are the oldest known of their kind and according to tradition they were a gift from the Governor of New Sweden, Johan Printz, to the then proprietor of Skokloster, Field Marshal Karl Gustav Wrangel. Photograph: The Royal Armoury.

The Conflict of the Estates and the Reduction

Sweden had become a Great Power, but her resources did not suffice to pay the troops and the government officials. The necessary funds were acquired by the State through the sale or transfer of crown lands and taxation rights to the Nobility. In consequence 600 noble families in the mid-Seventeenth Century possessed 72 per cent of the Swedish soil, only 28 per cent remaining in the hands of the Crown or of the peasant freeholders. This amounted to an overwhelming transfer of property. Practically everything Gustavus Vasa had taken from the Church had now come into the hands of the Nobility.

As a result most of the Swedish peasants had in one way or another become dependent on aristocratic landowners. Many peasant proprietors were obliged to pay their taxes to noblemen, making it difficult for them to assert their independence.

As late as the Sixteenth Century most of the nobility still lived on their estates close to the villages. Now it became more profitable for them to remove their property from the closed villages and to acquire large estates and manor farms. And so they began to build the stately castles and country houses described by Erik Dahlbergh in his work "Suecia antiqua et hodierna". The private dwellings they built for themselves had never before nor later existed in Sweden: Axel Oxenstierna's Tidö, Carl Gustav Wrangel's Skokloster and Magnus Gabriel De la Gardie's Läckö, to mention only three.

Labour was required for the construction work and management of the estates. The crofts offered a solution. Peas-

Läckö Castle is situated to the north of Lidköping on a peninsula in Lake Vänern. The castle, which has three courtyards and more than 200 rooms, assumed its present form in the Seventeenth Century when it was the property of Magnus Gabriel De la Gardie, the Chancellor of the Realm. Photograph: Astrid Bergman-Sucksdorf.

ants who could no longer afford to pay rent to the landowners could instead reside in the crofts built on the estates. Thereafter they could pay their rent in the form of daily labour on the land. Landowners were often entitled to impose taxes on several villages in the vicinity of their estates, the villagers being obliged to perform a stated amount of work for the landowners. This was a threat not only to the state, which was deprived of its income, but also to the Estate of the peasant freeholders.

The peasants protested against the loss of their rights at a Riksdag in Stockholm in 1650: "We are aware that in other lands the country folk are thralls. We fear that the same fate may befall ourselves, although we were born freemen." The mood was extremely bitter that year, because famine stalked the land and the roads were crowded with beggars. Many people died of starvation.

When the Peasants came to the Riksdag they found they were not alone. The Clergy and the Burghers supported their demands that the power of the Nobility should be broken and that the donated estates should be restored to the Crown. They did not achieve any major results, but the three non-noble estates had learned to work together and the social struggle was to continue.

Queen Christina was in a difficult position. She was highly gifted, read widely and maintained contact with leading European scholars. She gathered a small court of learned men in the palace in Stockholm. The most celebrated was the philosopher René Descartes. However, she was unable to solve the major social problems of her day, and her own situation became impossible when she was secretly converted to the Roman Catholic Church. She felt obliged to abdicate, but not until she had arranged for her cousin Charles Gustavus to be accepted as successor to the throne.

Nor did Charles X Gustavus find the time to tackle the major internal problems: controversies between the estates and the maintenance of the army. By means of a new war of conquest in Poland he hoped to find an outlet for social grievances and at the same time to supply his army on hostile territory. The Polish campaign went badly, and when the Danish King declared war on Sweden, Charles Gustavus turned on Denmark. He advanced into Jutland from the south, and during one of the boldest operations in military history he led his army across the frozen Belt and in 1658 imposed a peace which gave Sweden Scania, Blekinge, Halland and Bohuslän. Thereby Sweden acquired her permanent borders in the west and south.

Charles X Gustavus died two years later, and a lengthy regency government for his youthful son further confirmed the influence of the higher nobility. At the time ecclesiastical discipline was harsh in Sweden, and by means of warnings

Snaphane rifle, Göinge type, from the Snaphane guerilla district of Scania, mid-Seventeenth Century. The Royal Armoury.

from the pulpits concerning the omnipresence of the Devil the ground was prepared for numerous witchcraft trials. Several hundred people – mostly women – were executed as witches after they had been denounced by frightened villagers and forced to confess, sometimes after being tortured.

As soon as Charles XI had attained his majority he was obliged to fight a war against Denmark for the Scanian provinces. The decisive battle took place at Lund, where the King was victorious. During the four years the war lasted the Swedes had to fight a guerilla force of Scanian troops (*Snapphanar*) in the forested border region. After the Peace of 1679 Sweden retained the conquered provinces.

The year after the peace treaty the King and his councillors took action against the Regency Government. On the advice of the King the Riksdag determined that much of the lands held by the Nobility should be restored to the Crown. This reduction continued for many years and resulted in a total transformation of the social structure. Following the reduction Crown ownership had increased to 35.5 per cent, the peasant freemen held 31.5 per cent and the nobility only 33 per cent.

The aristocracy retained their ancestral estates and their privileged status, but the consequences of the reduction were nevertheless important: the peasants restored their independence and the Crown achieved stable finances.

The Decline of the Great Power

After the end of the Scanian War it was necessary for Charles XI to put the country on a peace footing as soon as possible. The Riksdag had granted him absolute power and it was possible for him to impose his will on the government of the entire country.

One of the major problems was the maintenance of the army in peacetime and of the fleet required to uphold the mastery of the Baltic Sea. A large proportion of the recovered crown property was assigned by the King to national defence.

With regard to the infantry, the peasants were exempted from the annual heavy conscription if they undertook to maintain an enlisted soldier. Charles XI's military organization, the *indelningsverk*, required that every province or county in war and peace should form and maintain a regular regiment of 1,200 men. The soldier received annual pay and in most cases a small croft to cultivate and live in.

In the case of the cavalry, the proprietors of independent farms undertook to provide a cavalryman, horse and equipment, being thereby exempted from taxation. Like the men of the Foot, the troopers received annual pay and a croft to live in.

The officers became officials. For them the only qualifications were efficiency and years of service. The King preferred his officers to rise from the ranks. Every officer was granted a farm to live in. About 3,000 officers' residences were spread over the country. Charles XI's *indelningsverk* was to survive for more than 200 years – until 1901. Many officers' quarters are still to be found – in private ownership.

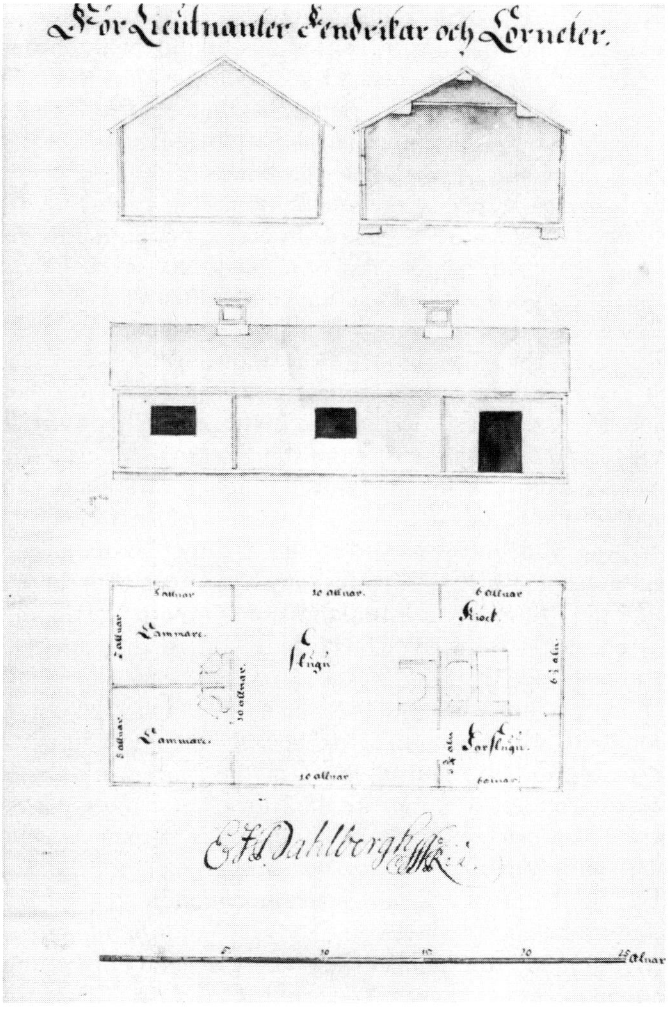

Uniform housing drawings for the thousands of officers' dwellings in Sweden and Finland were prepared by Quartermaster-General Erik Dahlbergh in Stockholm in the 1680's. This is what the quarters looked like for lieutenants, second-lieutenants and cornets of the Regular Army. The Military Archives, Stockholm.

Regular inspections were arranged for the regiments and provided Charles XI with continuous employment throughout the summers. He checked the uniforms and the equipment and supervised the training of the troops. Thus the army became a well-equipped and well-trained force at the King's disposal. In Blekinge the town of Karlskrona was established as a naval base and shipbuilding yard. In 1700 it contained 38 ships of the line with crews amounting to more than 15,000 men. The sailors were provided for in the same way as the troops with annual pay and crofts to live in.

The years of peace were a blessing for commerce. Sweden still supplied her own arms. The renowned Carolean sword was produced at various iron foundries. The iron industry made heavy demands on forestry, and in order to ensure that these demands could be met the state imposed severe restrictions. No ironworks was permitted to manufacture more than could be supplied by the annual yield of the local forests. As a result the iron smiths moved to the heavily forested areas of the Bergslagen district. In this way a number of large ironworks were founded in Värmland and Southern Norrland.

The men of Bergslagen, who had worked the iron ore in the mines since the Middle Ages, were succeeded by wealthy foundry owners who had the means to employ labour and extend the workings. Bar iron became the most important export commodity. During much of the Eighteenth Century Swedish iron was to dominate the European market and Britain was the principal customer, importing 90 per cent of its iron from Sweden.

During the reign of Charles XI the conquered provinces of the south became Swedicized. The change of nationality was carried out with the utmost skill. The University of Lund was founded in 1668 to make Swedes out of the former Danes and to train priests and officials for the conquered provinces. The children were requested to learn to read and write Swedish, and the clergy played an important part by preaching in Swedish. When war broke out in 1700 the Scanians served in their own regiments in the Swedish Army.

One of the numerous ironworks founded during the Seventeenth Century was Vira bruk in Roslagen. Its speciality was iron blade and it supplied the entire Carolean Army with swords. The company was still active in the 1930's. Vira bruk is the only plant which reveals how a Seventeenth Century ironworks looked. The picture shows us an interior of the smithy. Photograph: National Museum of Science and Technology.

Charles XI died in the midst of his restless labours in 1697, and his fifteen year old son Charles XII became King. While the late King was still lying in state in the palace, a great fire broke out which destroyed most of the buildings. This was thought to be an evil omen for the new reign.

In 1700 Sweden was attacked on three fronts simultaneously by Russia, Poland and Denmark, a carefully planned action to crush the power of Sweden. Charles XII immediately took the field with the Carolean Army. He defeated Denmark, while the Swedish fortresses in Estonia and Livonia held both the other aggressors at bay.

In a series of brilliant actions Charles XII beat the Russians at Narva in 1700 and the Poles at Kliszow in 1702. In 1707 Charles XII concluded peace with Poland at Altranstädt, and thereafter he aimed a mortal blow at Moscow, the heart of Russia. His campaign was a failure. The Swedish army was defeated at Poltava in 1707 and forced to capitulate.

For some years Charles XII remained in Turkey, where with partial success he tried to involve the Turks in the war. After his return to Sweden in 1714 he had to conduct a defensive war not only against his old adversaries but also against Britain-Hanover and Prussia. With the aid of his minister, Georg Heinrich von Görtz, he sought to play off Britain against Russia, but in the midst of these complicated diplomatic procedures he was killed by a bullet outside the fortress of Fredriksten in Norway on 30th November 1718. One month later 3,000 of his troops perished in a snowstorm in the Norwegian mountains.

After Charles XII's death Sweden had to conclude a number of peace treaties which brought about the collapse of Sweden as a Great Power. Russia took the Baltic provinces, and to the south of the Baltic Sea Sweden retained only a few small garrisons.

The Age of Freedom

After Charles XII's death the absolute monarchy was abolished. The new Constitution of 1719 placed power in the hands of the Riksdag. King and Council should implement the resolutions of the Riksdag. The Council had 16 members; its President became the real regent of the country. The Age of Freedom, as it was called, is associated with a development of Swedish political life. For the first time parliamentarianism, in many ways similar to the contemporary English model, began to play an important part. The Riksdag still consisted of four Estates which held their deliberations in separate chambers, had their own speakers, kept minutes of their meetings but conferred with each other from time to time.

The Nobility were represented by the heads of families. On certain occasions those present could number a thousand. The Nobles met in the House of the Nobility which, during the sessions of the Riksdag, became the centre of Swedish political life.

The Estate of the Clergy consisted of fifty members, made up of all the bishops and clergy appointed from every diocese. The Burghers represented 101 towns in Sweden and Finland. Stockholm appointed ten members, Gothenburg three and smaller towns one or two. Often various towns combined to appoint a single representative.This estate numbered 80 and 90 members.

For the Estate of the Peasants every rural district known as a *härad,* or hundred, elected one member of the Riksdag. Only peasant proprietors and crown tenants were eligible. The nobility's peasants were ineligible as were the large tenantless social groups of the countryside. This estate numbered about 150 members.

The Riksdag observed the majority principle: a resolution required the assent of three estates. Much of the power lay with the committees. The most important of these was the Secret Committee which dealt with foreign policy, defence and the national finances. The Peasants were ineligible for membership of this committee.

Two parties, the Hats and the Caps, were formed and strove for power. It was natural that these parties originally took form in the House of the Nobility. They broke through the barriers of the estates and had their own programmes, whips and political clubs. The Hats wished to support the rise of industry and sought the political aid of France to wreak vengeance upon Russia. The Caps protected agriculture. Their sympathies lay with Britain which was an important trading partner. Many members of the Riksdag found it hard to support themselves in Stockholm and received funds from the French, the British and even the Russian minister.

The Hats held power longest and twice involved Sweden in wars. During a war with Russia in 1741–1743 the Swedish army was forced to capitulate outside Helsingfors, and the eastern part of Finland was lost under the peace treaty. Another equally ill-prepared war against Prussia in 1757–1762 ended without any loss of territory.

In the 1740's the Riksdag granted funds for the construction of a large naval fortress in Finland, Sveaborg, in the skerries near Helsingfors. This fortress was built by thousands of soldiers under the command of Augustin Ehrensvärd. At this time hundreds of Swedish officers volunteered for service in foreign armies and navies in order to acquire experience. They participated in all the wars of the Eighteenth Century, including the American War of Independence.

The King was powerless, and when he refused to sign the resolutions of the Council, recourse was had to a royal signature stamp. While the majority of the nobility supported the

During the Eighteenth and Nineteenth Centuries Swedish iron cannons were a major export commodity. This 24-pounder was cast at a Swedish foundry in 1697. It weighs 3 tons. The Royal Army Museum, Stockholm.

policy of the Hats, towards the end of the period the Caps succeeded in uniting the three non-noble estates in opposition to the privileges of the aristocracy.

This was the Age of Enlightenment. Interest was concentrated on social, practical and useful matters. The individual was considered to be personally responsible for development. Everyone – each in his own way – should contribute to the economic welfare of the realm. Various opinions were now debated freely in a flora of journals and news sheets which began to be published at this time in Stockholm and other towns.

The Age of Freedom was, from the economic and cultural points of view, a golden age. Iron was Sweden's leading export commodity. By the middle of the Eighteenth Century there were 366 ironworks in the country and a total annual production of 47,000 tons of wrought-iron goods. The foundries had more or less the same working structure and architectural plan. The ironmaster and his family lived in a mansion where a special literary culture often flourished. From the mansion to the church the streets were straight and lined with the neat hourses of the ironsmiths and other workers. In many places these early examples of town-planning still survive.

Towns were founded and industry expanded. Commerce was all the fashion, and high customs duties were imposed to protect native enterprise from foreign competition. The textile industry employed 13,000–14,000 workers in all. The largest textile companies were located in Norrköping and Stockholm, while at Alingsås a woollen factory was established, of which the King and several Councillors of the Realm were part-owners. And yet only a small proportion of the population derived their income from industry. Scarcely one-tenth of the population resided in towns.

Agriculture was still by far the most important source of income. During the Eighteenth Century the population increased to 1.8 million in Sweden and to 400,000 in Finland. In order to support the growing population the Government recommended the cultivation of the outlying village lands. Various reforms were discussed with the aim of making agriculture more profitable.

Lappish arts and crafts are often distinguished by their beautiful decoration. Top: wooden box with carved decoration. Bottom: cheese receptacle with open-work decoration. Nordic Museum. Photo: Ulla Wåger.

The Government also supported the colonization of the northern wildernesses. The narrow coastal plain was Norrland's real agricultural district. The small coastal towns – Umeå, Piteå and Luleå – had been founded during the reign of Gustavus II Adolphus. Inland lay stretches of virgin country inhabited by Lapps, some of whom were nomads and lived of their herds of reindeer, others were more or less permanently settled. The Swedish Church maintained a mission for the Lapps. Annual markets in the Lapp villages provided trading opportunities with the outer world.

During the Eighteenth Century many young people made their way into the Lapp country in search of land. They came from the villages along the Norrland coast and were almost always very poor. The Government tempted them with

In the Palace Gardens at Drottningholm Adolphus Frederick built the elegant little China Palace for his Queen Lovisa Ulrika in 1753. It was an expression of the interest of the rococo period in Chinese art. The present castle was built in 1763–1769 to the design of C. F. Adelcrantz.

promises of exemption from taxes for fifteen years and other privileges. It was in the interests of the state that the wild lands should be cultivated. An increase of cultivated land meant an increase in revenues from taxation. There was also the hope that the pioneers could serve as a labour reserve for the Norrland mines.

In time the penetration of the virgin lands of the interior led to conflicts between the settlers and the Lapps. The basic issues were fishing waters and pastures for the reindeer. The law courts supported the settlers in almost every case, and the Lapps were forced to withdraw from the controversial areas.

During the Eighteenth Century travelling in Sweden was still something of an adventure. The roads were usually bad, and therefore the best time for travelling was the winter, when the numerous rivers were frozen and people could travel by sledge. The botanist Linnaeus, Sweden's scientific genius, was also an enthusiastic explorer who wrote detailed reports on the special characteristics of the provinces he visited. He more than anyone else taught the Swedes to experience Nature and its wonders in a new way.

To many people foreign trade seemed the most important way to prosperity. In 1731 a Swedish East India Company was founded in Gothenburg. There was a considerable demand for silk, tea and porcelain in Europe, and it was hoped that active participation in the trade with the East Indies would result in profit to Sweden, the commodities being imported directly into the country. Hopes ran high for the new company. Wealthy foreigners would be attracted to Sweden, young men would be trained as seamen and the Swedish shipbuilding yards would receive orders.

In 1732 the first ship, "Friedericus Rex", set sail from Gothenburg to Canton, the only Chinese port open to foreigners. The voyage proved a great success and extremely profitable for its backers. Some of the commodities were sold abroad. From that time until 1813, when the company was liquidated, 132 expeditions with 31 vessels were undertaken to the East Indies.

Interest in China and Chinese culture became intense and left its mark on the Swedish way of life. Chinese motifs blended with the new fashionable rococo style in a mood of carefree beauty. To many Swedish politicians China appeared to be an ideal state. The disciples of Linnaeus were granted free passage on the ships of the East India Company and sent home reports on their travels and collections of animals and plants from the Far East. The whole world lay open to these young scholars. Per Kalm travelled to North America, Peter Forsskål to Arabia, and Anders Sparrman took part in James Cook's second expedition to the South Seas. Their experiences were fully recorded.

Queen Lovisa Ulrika's Palace Theatre at Drottningholm was built in 1754. Its golden age was during the reign of Gustavus III. It has achieved world fame on account of its authentic auditorium and well-preserved Eighteenth Century decorations and stage machinery. Photograph: O. Ekberg, Drottningholm Theatre Museum.

The Gustavian Era

After the death of Adolphus Frederick in 1771 his son Gustavus III ascended to the throne. He was now 24 years of age, precocious, imaginative and ambitious. His contemporaries reported that he found it a simple matter to win people to his side and that he displayed great skill in concealing his real feelings and thoughts.

The party controversies continued in the Riksdag, certainly stimulated by the general disquiet in Europe. The three non-noble estates desired equality and the abolition of the privileges of the nobility. In these aims they were supported by the Caps. The most aggressive estate was that of the peasantry, who had built up a permanent organization during the Age of Freedom. Many of its members had been trained in local government, in the village councils and rural courts, and almost all of them were literate.

The peasants considered that they had been ill-treated by the other estates and they now demanded places on the Secret Committee and even on the Council. At the Riksdag of 1772 the Caps assumed power. There was trouble in the country districts, and famine threatened in consequence of a bad harvest. The evil times caused many people to place their trust in the youthful King. The peasants believed that he would liberate them from the oppression of the nobility, while many aristocrats hoped that he would protect them and prevent a political revolution.

After his accession Gustavus III made several attempts to reconcile the parties. At the same time he worked intensively to broaden his popularity without conceding any promises. He was strongly in sympathy with enlightened despotism, and sought aid from the French Government to establish a similar constitution in Sweden.

On 19th August 1772 he followed the Guards to the Palace, where he addressed the officers of the Life Guards, who swore an oath of loyalty to him. He then locked up the members of the Council, drove away the Secret Committee and carried out a bloodless revolution. He and his followers wore a white armband, and the King himself rode into the city where he was hailed by rejoicing crowds. In a speech he declared that he wanted to be "first citizen among a free people". The poet Carl Michael Bellman praised him in a song, "A toast to Gustavus, the finest King in all the northern lands!"

All opposition broke down throughout the country. Two days after the coup d'état the Riksdag was summoned to the Palace. Following a stately speech, the King read a new constitution which was accepted by those present. This provided that the King should govern the country. The influence of the Council was reduced. The Riksdag should be summoned at the King's discretion, and its powers were also curtailed. As a result of his revolution the King stopped foreign intervention in Swedish political life. Great Britain accepted the coup d'état, while Russia was fully occupied with the first partition of Poland.

The Secret Committee vanished for ever, and there were

Gustavus III's new 'riksdaler', minted in 1777, may be seen at the Royal Coin Cabinet. Photograph: ATA.

now no Riksdag parties. The King dealt gently with his opponents, and members of the Hat and Cap parties were included in his government. The freedom of the press was limited. Discussion of foreign policy and of the constitution was forbidden, and to win the favour of the clergy the King also prohibited all discussion of the Established Church and religious matters.

Important reforms were carried out. One of the earliest measures was a reform of the coinage which benefited all social classes. Sweden introduced a silver coinage. The 'riksdaler' became the principal coin, and the 'riksdaler' of Gustavus III was the most beautiful coin ever minted in Sweden.

The King also implemented a far-reaching reform of the bureaucracy. Government servants were now entitled to retire with pay at the age of 70 – previously they had to work until they died. More open to discussion was the King's intervention in the matter of aquavit. During the Eighteenth Century aquavit had become the national drink. Everyone drank it – young and old, rich and poor. The servants in the country were entitled to their morning dram, and the troops received their ration in cold weather. Every peasant distilled aquavit at home for his domestic needs. Now the King forbade all such domestic distilling and instead he introduced a state aquavit monopoly. This new ordinance aroused powerful resistance, and home distilling was once again permitted in 1798.

During the Age of Freedom the aristocracy dominated the cultural life of Sweden. The most remarkable cultural figure was Carl Gustaf Tessin, the Palace Architect, who collected beautiful works of art at his country estate of Åkerö in Södermanland. His paintings are now preserved in the National Museum, while his collection of medals have been incorporated in the Royal Cabinet of Coins and Medals.

Stately homes were constructed throughout the country. The most splendid of all was Övedskloster in Scania, built to the orders of the far-seeing landowner Hans Ramel.

After Gustavus III's revolution the non-noble estates

Silver coffee pot dating from 1764 made by J. Bergengren, Kristianstad. Röhsska Museum of Arts and Crafts in Gothenburg.

began to flourish, and a burger middle-class set its mark on cultural life. Gustavus III became the supreme arbiter of taste, and all the recognized artists worked for him and received his support. This middle class form of culture was national. The King wished to create a Swedish theatre. He participated in the writing of several plays and ordered the building of a magnificent opera house in Stockholm. He also introduced a national dress inspired by the traditional Swedish national costume.

In 1786 the King founded the Swedish Academy to create a rich and modern language. Swedish art reached its zenith with the painters Carl Gustaf Pilo and Alexander Roslin as well as the sculptor Johan Tobias Sergel. A special Gustavian style exerted its influence on internal decoration, furniture and silverware.

During the Eighteenth Century mortality was extremely high in Stockholm, where consumption raged in the crowded tenement blocks and epidemics frequently broke out. Hospitals began to be constructed – the earliest being the Hospital of the Seraphim in 1752.

In 1772 there were schools in 10 per cent of all the parishes. In the towns there were schools which taught reading and arithmetic to the children of the middle-class. In some towns there were schools which consisted of several classes and from which the pupils could proceed to secondary schools and the university. There were also private schools in the towns for the children of the rich and these were attended by both boys and girls. Not all the children attended school.

Gustavus III did much to strengthen the Navy and reinforced the fleets of warships and galleys which were intended to protect the coasts and skerries. Among many splendid new vessels was the frigate "Bellona", of which a model is preserved at the National Maritime Museum in Stockholm. Photograph: Nat. Mar. Mus.

Many peasant children worked on the farm, other children became craftsmen and workers in industry. Child-labour was long regarded as advantageous to the country and good training for youth.

On the initiative of Gustavus III a Swedish colony was established in the West Indies. During a visit to Paris in 1784 the King succeeded in making arrangements for Sweden to take over the small island of St Barthélemy. The previous year Sweden had signed a treaty of friendship and commerce with the United States of North America, thereby becoming the first of the neutral states of Europe to recognize the young republic. The King hoped that the West Indian colony would become a market for Swedish iron in the New World.

Gustavus III pursued a policy of reconciliation with Russia for a long time. During the North American War of Independence Sweden cooperated with Denmark and Russia in a league of armed neutrality for the protection of trade. At the same time the King invested heavily in the eastern defences of the country. He raised new military units in Finland, armed the naval forces at Karlskrona and built a special fleet of armed galleys based on the naval fortress of Sveaborg.

Gradually, as the King's rule became increasingly arbitrary, opposition grew, especially among the politically competent nobility who no longer played a decisive part in the development of society. In the Riksdag of 1786 the King encountered severe and purposeful opposition from all quarters. To deal with the internal discontent and to regain his popularity, the King reached the bold decision to start a war against Russia in 1788.

His plans failed. In Finland some hundred officers formed the Anja League, condemned the war and demanded peace negotiations. Simultaneously with this officers' mutiny Denmark declared war against Sweden. The situation was chaotic, but the King kept his head. He returned to Sweden and followed in Gustavus Vasa's footsteps to Dalecarlia, where he addressed the peasants at Mora.

Royalist feelings were immediately aroused and with their

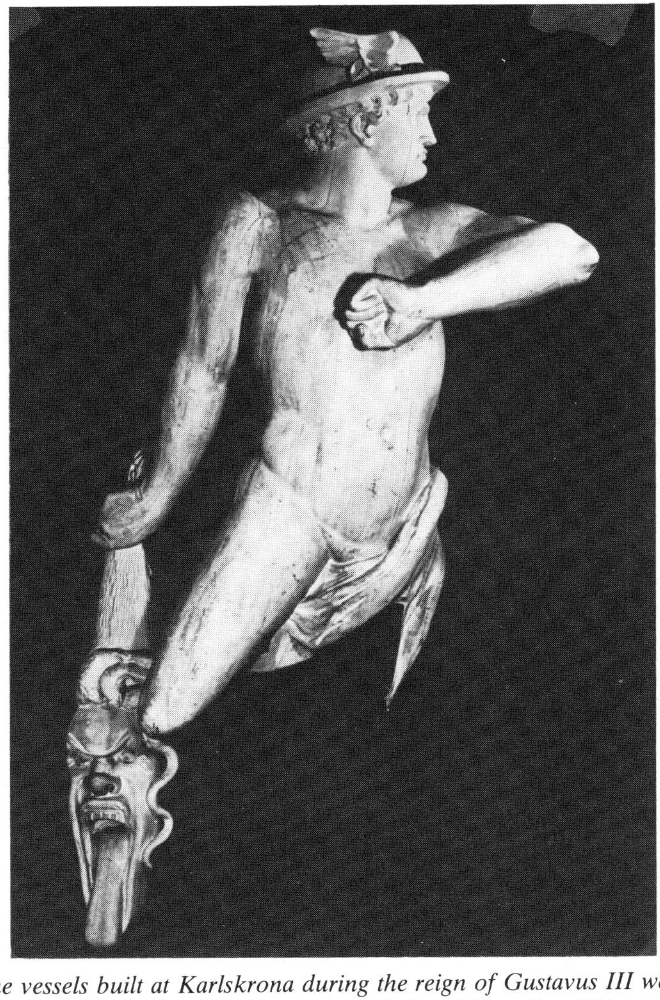

The vessels built at Karlskrona during the reign of Gustavus III were fitted with figureheads by the sculptor Johan Törnström. This statue of the god Hermes adorned the ship-of-the-line "Försiktigheten" which with its 60 guns took part in all the naval battles during the War of 1788–90 with Russia. The Naval Museum at Karlskrona contains an entire gallery with figureheads carved by Johan Törnström and his son Emanuel.

help the King took rapid action. The Anjala conspirators were arrested and the Riksdag was summoned to Stockholm in February 1789. The King sought the help of the non-noble estates who helped him to enforce an "Act of Union and Security" which gave him virtually unlimited powers, but in recompense deprived the nobility of their most important privileges. All had now equal rights to most appointments and the peasants were now permitted to purchase crown lands. These reforms, implemented some months before the French Revolution, implied a social revolution and contributed to the political and economic advance of the peasantry into the Nineteenth Century.

War against Russia continued. In the final decisive naval engagement at Svensksund on 9th July 1790, the Swedish Navy won perhaps its greatest victory. Peace was signed shortly afterwards without loss of territory.

Opposition to the King went underground. A group of officers and officials saw a solution in tyrannicide. At a fancy dress ball at the Opera House on 16th March 1792 Gustavus III was shot by an officer, Jacob Johan Anckarström. Two weeks later the King died.

Under Gustavus III's son, Gustavus IV Adolphus, Sweden became involved in the war against Napoleon. In 1803 Sweden entered into an alliance with Britain, her principal trading partner and Napoleon's great adversary. As Gustavus IV Adolphus refused to be drawn into the commercial blockade against Britain, in February 1808 Russian troops attacked across the Finnish border. Sveaborg surrendered and the Swedish-Finnish army was defeated. In the Peace of 1809 Sweden lost Finland, the eastern part of the realm. Stockholm was no longer the heart of the kingdom and the centre of gravity moved southwards and westwards.

Gustavus IV Adolphus was made the scapegoat for these misfortunes. He was deposed, driven into exile and died in 1837 at St Gallen in Switzerland. His uncle Charles XIII succeeded to the throne, but the Gustavian absolute monarchy was abolished.

Gustavus III was murdered at a fancy dress ball at the Roual Opera House in Stockholm on 16th March 1792 by a group of aristocratic members of the opposition with radical ideas of equality. The King was dressed in the so-called Swedish costume with a Venetian cloak, but he was easily recognizable on account of the Orders of the Seraphim and the Sword which he wore on his jacket. Photograph: Svärdström.

Charles XIV John and Liberalism

The equality with respect to privilege resulting from the French Revolution in the course of a series of violent upheavals reached Sweden by means of a lengthy process of peaceful revolutions under Gustavus Vasa, Charles XI and Gustavus III. The peasants were permitted to purchase their crofts, the common people were entitled to buy the land of the nobility and to occupy the high offices of government.

The new constitution adopted in 1809, the year after the fall of Gustavus IV Adolphus, was to remain the basis of Swedish government for 162 years. It was built on historic tradition and experience; and it aimed at achieving a balance between the various organs of state. The King alone should govern the country, but before making his decisions he was to take advice from a Council of State of nine members appointed by himself. The Councillors should be responsible for their advice to the Riksdag. Legislative power was divided between the monarch and the Riksdag, while the right to tax lay with the Riksdag. The judiciary power consisted of judges who could not be dismissed. A special judicial commissioner was appointed to safeguard the rights of citizens against the bureaucracy.

Since Charles XIII was childless, the Riksdag resolved to offer the crown to a Danish prince, Christian August of Augustenborg, but he died of a stroke in Scania in 1810. A rumour spread that the Gustavians had poisoned him. At his funeral in Stockholm one of the leading Gustavians, Axel von Fersen, Marshal of the Realm, followed immediately after the coffin. Fersen, who was renowned for his attempt to rescue the King and Queen of France during the Revolution, was attacked by the mob and murdered without the troops on parade making the slightest attempt to intervene.

Jean Baptiste Bernadotte, one of Napoleon's marshals, was now declared successor to the throne. In Sweden he adopted the names Karl Johan. On his arrival in Sweden he immediately assumed direction of the affairs of the country, persuading the Riksdag to strengthen the national defence by introducing general conscription in addition to the regular army. In 1812 he signed an alliance with Russia against Napoleon. In 1813 he took part in the campaign in Germany but spared the Swedish troops. Afterwards he forced the Danes to give up Norway in exchange for Swedish Pomerania, the sole surviving conquest from the Great Power era. As Norway protested and adopted a free constitution of her own, the Swedes had to intervene with armed force. This was Sweden's last war and it ended with the Swedish-Norwegian Union of 1814. Norway retained her free constitution and was granted home rule.

Thanks to these military successes, Charles John revived the nation's self-confidence after the catastrophes in Finland, and under his continuously consistent peace policy the basis was laid for major developments in the fields of commerce and culture. After he became King in 1818 under the name of Charles XIV John, he created considerable confidence in himself as a person and this benefited the monarchy as a whole.

In his foreign policy Charles XIV John built up amicable relations with both Russia and Britain without committing the country to any alliances. Thus it was during his reign that traditional Swedish neutrality policy began to take shape.

Developments in Western Europe, and above all the industrial revolution in Britain during the late Eighteenth Century, resulted in increased demands for grain for bread on all the major markets. The effects of these trends were also felt in Sweden. In order to exploit the good times with rising prices for grain, the Government and the landowners brought about a complete reorganization of agriculture. It

At the village of Eriksöre on the west coast of Öland the long village street has been preserved. Photograph: The Nordic Museum.

began on the estate of Svaneholm in Scania, where Rutger Maclean, inspired by Danish models, demolished the old villages on the estate and replaced them with isolated farms. Thereby he obtained better possibilities of exploiting the lands of the estate by means of new methods.

The good results at Svaneholm inspired others. In 1803 Gustavus IV Adolphus enacted an agricultural reform for Scania, which was followed in 1827 by a resolution aimed at improving agriculture everywhere in Sweden. This meant the end of the large villages. A highly differentiated cultural pattern based on fellowship and cooperation now vanished from the scene.

These agricultural reforms were followed by others and during the years 1805–1815 agricultural land increased by 15 per cent. The cultivation of grain continued to expand so that in normal years Sweden was able to feed her growing population. This population remained in the countryside, and from the beginning of the Nineteenth Century there was a growing proletariat of landless persons who posed a serious problem in the rural districts.

The peasants made diligent use of their possibilities to purchase their own farms. In 1825 more than half the farms were in the hands of peasant proprietors. Many societies worked to make agriculture more profitable. The ploughs were improved, and the farmers learned to raise cattle in accordance with new methods. One novelty was the cultivation of potatoes. For the rural proletariat the potato was a staple diet. The potato became very popular when the farmers discovered that it could be used to produce aquavit, while the draff could serve as sustenance for cattle.

During and after the Napoleonic Wars Sweden enjoyed a brilliant era associated with literature and research. The men who created this golden age were university graduates and the sons of ironmasters, clergy and burghers – the middle-class had now assumed responsibility for culture. They were also devoted to their home regions. Esaias Tegnér and Erik Gustaf Geijer came from Värmland and the psalmist Johan Olof Wallin was a native of Dalecarlia, while the Stockholmer Carl Jonas Love Almquist in his novels made much of the countryside in the vicinity of the capital.

At the same time Jöns Jacob Berzelius, one of the world's leading chemists, was working at the newly founded Royal Caroline Institute in Stockholm. He became the great constructor of chemical systems and created the language of formulae for basic substances still in use today.

After the loss of Finland Sweden's military situation was completely changed. Despite the peace policy of Charles XIV John, it was realized that the only potential danger came from Russia. The new defence plan was based on central defence. If the enemy made a landing on the east coast of Sweden, the army would fight a series of delaying actions while withdrawing inland towards a central fortress situated on the Göta Canal. The fortress, which was built on the shore of Lake Vänern, was named Karlsborg, and it was agreed that in the event of war the Royal Family, the Government and the National Bank of Sweden should move to the fortress. For ninety years work was concentrated on this fortress, but meanwhile the world was changing. The notion of central defence was abandoned in favour of frontier defence. Railways were constructed and linked the various parts of the country, and in 1900 work began on the construction of the fortress of Boden, near the Finnish border, which was to

At the Berzelius Museum on the premises of the Royal Swedish Academy of Sciences in Stockholm we can study the life and work of the great chemist. This picture shows the cupboard where he kept his preparations and some of the glassware he used for his experiments.

replace Karlsborg.

As late as the beginning of the 1840's there were still many ironworks in the Bergslagen district. Characteristic of these was their antiquated technology and low production. The industry was subjected to numerous government regulations. It was impossible to start a new ironworks. The production of iron was constant, but the market was threatened. During the Napoleonic wars, the British – Sweden's principal customer – had discovered a way of producing bar iron by means of pit coal instead of charcoal, and had thus become independent of Swedish supplies. When Britain was lost as a customer Sweden continued to export iron to the United States, but future prospects seemed highly uncertain.

In the 1830's enterprising ironmasters in Bergslagen succeeded in devising a method of greatly improving the quality of the iron and at the same time of increasing production. The changeover to this method, the Lancashire process, involved heavy costs, which were beyond the means of the smaller ironworks. Thus the Lancashire process contributed to a reorganization and concentration of the iron industry.

The far-sighted iron masters were converts to British Liberal ideas. They wished to abolish the Government domination of their industry and to achieve the maximum possible flexibility in order to compete with foreign industry. In the 1830's there began a series of conflicts between Conservatives and Liberals in the Riksdag and in the press. The middle-class, consisting of investors in industry, business men, landowners and publicists, furiously attacked officialdom, demanding the abolition of all ordinances and advocating a change in the composition of the Riksdag so that it could stand for the new society of the middle-class.

In Stockholm the mouthpiece of the Liberals was the newspaper Aftonbladet, founded during the July Revolution of 1830 by Lars Johan Hierta. Two years later Gothenburg also acquired a Liberal newspaper, Göteborgs Handels- och Sjöfarts Tidning.

The opposition won no decisive victories during the reign of

An old school house at Takstens gård in the parish of Lärbro on Gotland. The teacher lived on the top floor, the bottom floor was the classroom. The children sat on benches along the long walls of the room. Photograph: The Nordic Museum.

Charles XIV John, but an important reform was implemented in 1842. This referred to education. It was now resolved that there should be at least one elementary school in every parish and that all children should be taught reading, writing and arithmetic. The construction of schools took some time. There were no regular teaching hours and textbooks were in short supply. The teacher was to be paid by the parish. Teachers' salaries were low, but the teachers were aware of their cultural task and worked hard for the new liberal ideas. In this way many of them became pioneers for the democratic development of society.

Emigration and Industrialization

During the years 1800–1850 the population of Sweden increased from 2.3 to 3.5 million. Relatively this was the greatest increase in population Sweden had hitherto undergone. Mortality rapidly declined while the birth-rate remained on the whole unchanged. Contributory factors to this development were the long period of peace combined with improved medical care and more nourishing food, above all as the result of the increased cultivation of potatoes.

Not all the social classes increased equally. The proportion of the urban population was unchanged, about 10 per cent. The marked increase in the population took place in the rural areas. This increase was considerable in all counties, but especially so in the Norrland counties – due to colonization – as well as in Scania and the West of Sweden, where agriculture had improved markedly as a result of the new methods recently introduced.

The increase was most noticeable in the case of the poorer classes, crofters, labourers, cotters and others. Many were descended from peasants. To a considerable extent the farmers' sons received their share of the farms by the splitting up of homesteads, but such parcelling of the land could not be driven beyond a certain point, and the population was growing more rapidly than the parcelling permitted.

While the peasants were rising in society and were to form a politically influential middle-class, many of their descendants sank into the mass of the poor and landless. The social gap between peasant proprietors and the agricultural proletariat grew wider. By 1850 40 per cent of the population belonged to the landless proletariat.

Cottars had very little in the way of fields and meadows. This crofter's cottage with a thatched roof was moved from Blekinge to Skansen in Stockholm. Photograph: The Nordic Museum.

The population explosion in the countryside became the most serious social problem during the first half of the Nineteenth Century. The poorer classes lived under straitened circumstances. When harvests were poor, landowners and farmers had to get rid of some of their servants and labourers, and many of these were forced to wander about begging in the parishes. When famine threatened, many found their way to the towns, where fever and sickness took their heavy toll of the already undernourished.

One solution to this otherwise insoluble social problem was emigration. Already in the 1840's individual Swedes had made their way to North America. Pamphlets and newspaper articles circulated about this land of liberty and equality, where there were no landowners, clergy or bailiffs. Letters from America passed from hand to hand. During the 1850's large numbers of Swedes emigrated to the New World in the

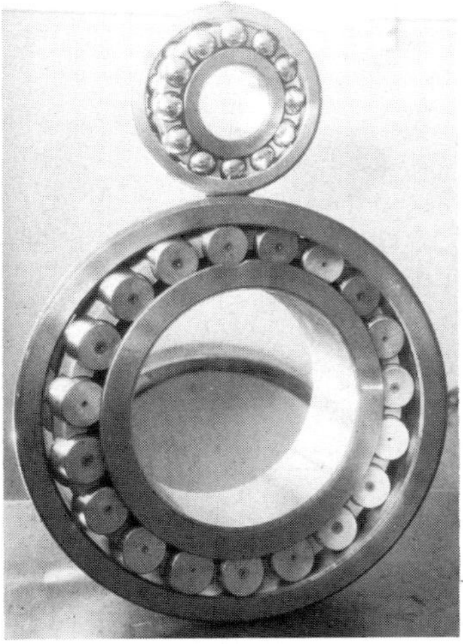

Three of the inventions which have made Swedish industry famous throughout the world – the ball-bearing, the separator and the Primus stove. They can be studied at the National Museum of Science and Technology in Stockholm, where different departments display the development of Swedish industry and the science of engineering.

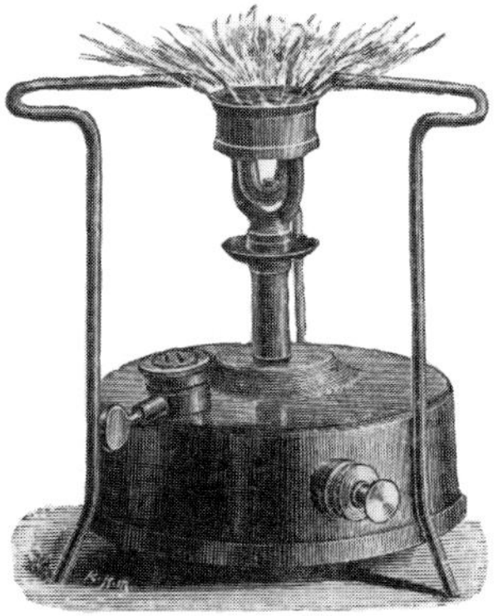

west to find land of their own to cultivate. In years when the crops failed their number expanded.

Emigration was to continue until the 1920's. It is estimated that during these seventy years some 1.2 million Swedes emigrated, mainly to the United States. There they spread over the whole of the Middle West and settled in the wide open spaces of Iowa, Wisconsin, Minnesota, Kansas and Nebraska. In time their settlements took on a profoundly Swedish character with their own schools, churches, mission chapels and newspapers. Many Swedes stayed in the cities – in Chicago, which became the big Swedish city, but also in New York, Minneapolis, and Seattle on the west coast.

Gradually Sweden was able to take care of her own surplus population. The poor in rural areas abandoned their crofts and were recruited into the new industries. In Sweden industry was a late phenomenon. As late as 1850 only 10 per cent of the population earned their daily bread from mining and other industries. But conditions were promising for an industrial break-through at that time. Complete commercial freedom had been implemented. Mechanical technology was on the march. There was no shortage of labour. Railways and steamships had improved communications, and several commercial banks had been established to supply credit to industry. But still more important was a change of attitude on the part of people. The mood was one of optimism, of faith that a Golden Age awaited an active generation.

The earliest factories were built for the cotton industry, which was mainly located in Västergötland, and was for a long time operated as a rural craft with agents who ordered the goods, and salesmen who sold them throughout the country. As a result of British influence spinning was mechanized, and from the 1830's factories were built with spinning and weaving machines.

Far more workers were employed in the heavy woollen industry which had its centre in Norrköping. Here, too, weaving in peasant homes had long been a secondary source of income after agriculture. In the 1870's the earliest large textile firms made their first appearance. Their activities rapidly expanded, thanks to increased demand in the country. Machine-woven materials replaced manual and brought about a trend for mass-production of clothes and greater uniformity.

The industrial revolution in Western Europe created an enormous demand for timber for the workers' houses in the towns. In the first instance this timber was supplied by Norway, but from the 1850's onwards Sweden also had a timber industry. A technical invention made it possible to make use of steam and establish steam sawmills at the mouths of rivers. Timber was floated down the rivers, sawn in the estuaries and then dispatched after drying directly by sea.

Norrland became the land of the future and capital flowed in from Southern Sweden and abroad. Hundreds of sawmills were constructed. Speculators bought huge areas of forest from the peasants for almost nothing and caused great damage to the forests. From 1850 until 1870 the export of timber increased by 500 per cent – more than 40 per cent of Sweden's exports consisted of timber.

In the 1870's Swedish technicians were making great efforts to produce wood and paper pulp by chemical means. The great age of the cellulose industry began twenty years later. Its centre was located in Norrland. Special sulphite factories were built to meet the ever-growing demands for newsprint. At the same time the companies began to apply far-sighted methods to conserve the supply of timber.

In the iron industry, too, great changes took place in the late Nineteenth Century. The Limited Liability Companies' Act of 1848 made it easier for companies to acquire capital. Technological advances made it possible to produce steel in large quantities at cheap prices. The small foundries disappeared, the entire production being concentrated in a few large ironworks, around which new communities grew up.

Iron exports increased rapidly. At the same time specialization began in what had hitherto been a uniform industry. A mechanical manufacturing industry flourished in the 1890's and was soon established on the world market. Swedish inventions often paved the way for development. Ball-bearings, separators, the Primus stove, matches and AGA lights – all would soon be major articles for the export market.

Electrification played an important part. As early as the 1860's electric lighting was tried out in the towns. The primary energy for these small plants was supplied by steam engines and not hydro-power. But water would soon recover its old role as the source of energy for industry. At the end of the 1880's Jonas Wennström, a genius inventor, solved the problem of the transmission of power by means of the electrical three-phase system. In 1906 the Government decided to make its debut as a producer of power. About the same time

Sweden's earliest locomotive, "Förstlingen" ("The First"), was built in 1853 by Munktells Mechanical Workshops at Eskilstuna. A model of this locomotive is preserved at the Railway Museum at Gävle where numerous objects illustrate the history of railways.

numerous municipal and private power companies were founded. Technological development brought about cooperation between state, municipal and private power distribution, in the course of which Sweden became electrified.

The new communications linked all parts of Sweden. In 1854 the Riksdag determined that railways should be constructed in Sweden. The State would be responsible for the main lines with the aid of capital from abroad, while municipalities and private companies were given a free hand to construct local railways. In this way the country acquired an extensive railway network. Around the railway stations entire new communities grew up: Katrineholm, Hallsberg, Nässjö, Hässleholm and others.

Simultaneously, steam engines helped to revolutionize travel by sea. By the 1860's steamships began to outclass sailing vessels. Ten years later Sweden had her first steamship lines. Shipbuilding yards emerged from the mechanical workshop industry. The first shipyards to specialize in the construction of steamers were the Götaverken and Eriksberg yards in Gothenburg and Kockums in Malmö. Not until the Twentieth Century did Sweden have regular transoceanic steamship traffic.

Postal and telephone services were other important means of communication for the growth of industrialism. The first stamps were issued in Sweden in 1855, and thus a uniform rate was established for the entire country. By the end of the 1880's the State-owned Department of Telecommunications had begun to establish a nationwide telephone network. The inventor L.M.Ericsson designed a practical table model which served to popularize the telephone very rapidly.

From the 1870's onwards a steady flow of agricultural labourers, crofters and servants transferred to the new industries which absorbed much of the surplus population. In 1870 15 per cent of the population was engaged in industry and handicrafts. Sweden now had 80,000 industrial workers. By 1900 there were more than 300,000.

The hours of work were long, in most industries more than

Sweden's first stamp, 1855. The uniform postal rate for the whole country was 4 skilling banco. The Postal Museum in Stockholm contains stamps from Sweden and other countries as well as a big library of philately and postal history. Photograph: Yngve Hellström.

12 hours. Most of the work was manual – dragging, towing and carrying. Work was heavy and wages were low. In the course of industrial expansion the workers' houses were inadequate and overcrowded. At the mines and sawmills many workers and their families were accommodated in barracks of several storeys, where they sometimes had at their disposal one room and a kitchen, sometimes only a kitchen.

Women and children were also employed in industry. For them, too, the working day was 12 hours long. Already by the 1870's women numbered one-fourth of the labour force. The majority were employed in the textile industry. Until the turn of the century their numbers increased at the same rate as the men's.

In almost all industries children were employed on the simpler tasks. As early as the 1850's discussions were held in the Riksdag on how the State could intervene to protect the workers, and in the first instance children, employed in industry. In 1852 the Riksdag passed a first act to prohibit night work in factories and workshops for minors under 18 years of age. This act could not be enforced in practice, but nevertheless it introduced the modern phase of labour safety legislation and social policy in Sweden.

The Major Popular Movements

The years 1850–1920 constituted the golden age of the popular movements in Sweden. It was during this period that Sweden was transformed from an agricultural society into an industrial country. During these times of change movement took place among the population. The population increased from 3.5 to nearly 6 million, but the surplus population no longer remained in the rural areas. The agricultural poor abandoned their crofts and made their way, never to return, to the emigrant ships and the new industries. The railways ended the rural isolation. People grew closer to each other. By far the greater part of the population lacked the franchise. But now they found new possibilities of improving their possibilities and influencing the community as a whole.

The 1850's saw the great break-through of the religious revivalist movement. It swept irresistibly over the entire country. No area was left unaffected, and it won adherents in all social classes. It was not under the direction of the clergy, but found most of its preachers among the laity. It was this democratic basis which made the revivalist movement the earliest major popular movement in Sweden.

The background of this movement is probably to be sought in the agricultural reforms and the break-up of the old villages. As long as the village existed, people were accustomed to attend their own church where the priest was the representative of the parish in the eyes of authority. The agricultural reforms destroyed the old ecclesiastical culture. When people moved to the outlying lands they lost the habit of mass-attendance at church. Their religious longings encouraged the colonizers to seek a more personal faith. They felt at

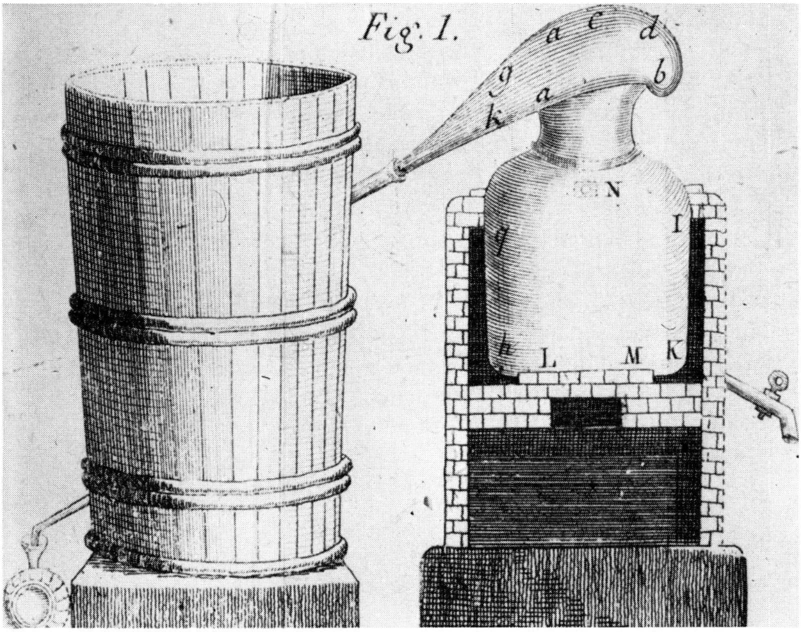

Aquavit distilling apparatus from the Eighteenth Century. Aquavit was considered a necessity of life, but only those who owned land were entitled to distil it. The landless were forbidden to do so. The Wine and Distillery Museum, Stockholm.

home in the new religious movements which covered the entire country. The old national church was weakened. It was admittedly to survive as the Established Church, but it was no longer the only ecclesiastical organization and people were entitled to secede from it and form their own congregations. Not until 1951 was an act passed granting freedom of religion in Sweden.

During the first half of the Nineteenth Century the Swedish people indulged in alcohol on an unprecedented scale. In 1829 there were no less than 173,000 aquavit-distilling machines in the country. Virtually every farm was a tavern. The consumption of strong spirits was enormous. In the 1820's consumption was estimated at 46 litres per inhabitant and year, compared with about 9 litres today. Everyone drank: the peasants, their farm-hands, the milkmaids and the landless labourers.

A powerful popular movement arose against the drinking of alcohol. Its leader was Peter Wieselgren, a vicar of the Established Church. He won numerous adherents all over the country. Distilling machines declined rapidly in number, and at the same time the consumption of spirits was reduced. In 1853 opinion had veered so strongly that the Government passed an aquavit act that strictly limited the right to distil

At Lennartsfors in the Parish of Trankil, Värmland, this building was erected in 1906–1907 as the Community Centre and IOGT lodge. Photograph: The Nordic Museum.

spirits. During the Twentieth Century the Swedish Temperance Movement has concentrated its efforts mainly on positive measures, information and effective temperance care. The movement became a powerful pressure group in the Riksdag and provided good training for many future politicians. Nowadays the sale of spirits, wines and strong beer is exclusively in the hands of a state-owned company.

The third great popular movement was the Labour Movement. The first trade unions were formed already in the 1870's. They grew up as necessary organizations and as an expression of the workers' dissatisfaction with the economic conditions. They grew into fighting organizations directed against employers, and their very basis was the solidarity of the workers. When Social Democracy was introduced into Sweden in the 1880's it became the political creed of the Labour Movement.

Strong popular movements arose to create opinion in favour of the universal franchise and social reforms. In 1898 the trade unions merged into a central organization covering the entire country. The same year it was decided that the members of the trade unions should be collectively associated with the Social Democratic Party; the individual was, however, free to leave the party.

In 1902 the employers also formed a common organization, the Swedish Employers' Confederation. Three years later the workers' and employers' organisations reached an agreement which recognized the freedom of association but with a compromise which proved highly controversial: the employer was entitled to engage and dismiss workers freely.

Other popular movements were formed during this dramatic decade. One concerned cooperation between workers and farmers, another was the Athletics Federation which grew up among the new popular groups created by industrialism.

Foreign Policy and Defence

During the reign of Charles XIV John neutrality became the guiding star of Swedish foreign policy. Personally the King had been strongly pro-Russian since the years of peace and he supported the Czar in the Polish Wars of Independence in 1830–1831. The King's pro-Russian attitude was not popular in Sweden, and opposition in the realm was instead aligned with Britain, whose ideas of freedom made her a model for the Swedish Liberals.

The 1830's witnessed a marked growth of pan-Scandinavianism among students and intellectuals. Sweden and Norway were linked in a union with a common King and foreign policy. To many people this union seemed only a beginning to a still greater union. Scandinavian scholars had already begun to cooperate. In 1839 graduates from all three Scandinavian countries gathered together at a big students' meeting in Copenhagen. This was the birth of political Scandinavianism.

While Charles John was against any idea of change in the Nordic Countries, his son and successor Oscar I was interested in the possibilities Scandinavianism offered to increase the political influence of Sweden. During the Danish-German War of 1848–1850 the Riksdag resolved at the suggestion of Oscar I to send 15,000 Swedish and Norwegian men to defend Denmark.

When an Anglo-French fleet entered the Baltic Sea during the Crimean War in 1854 Oscar saw a possiblity of recovering Finland from Russia. He abandoned his father's pro-Russian policy and in November 1855 he signed a treaty with the Western Powers, who promised him help in the event of a

Russian attack on his countries. The November Treaty, a direct departure from the policy of neutrality, remained in force until the beginning of the Twentieth Century. Sweden was to gain one advantage from the treaty: at the Peace of 1856 Russia undertook not to fortify the Åland Islands.

Oscar died in 1859. Under his son and successor Charles XV Scandinavianism became a major political question. In 1863 he offered the Danish King Frederick VII a military alliance and promised to come to the assistance of Denmark with 20,000 men in the event of a German attack. But personal royal power was on the decline, and the Swedish and Norwegian governments adopted a very much more cautious attitude to foreign policy than the King did.

When Prussia and Austria returned to the attack the following year, the Danes had to fight alone together with a small contingent of Swedish and Norwegian volunteers. Scandinavianism had failed, but cooperation between the Scandinavian peoples was to continue under different forms. At the beginning of the 1870's a new coinage system of crowns and öre was introduced simultaneously in all three countries.

Swedish defence was based essentially on the enlisted regular army with a strength of 23,000 men. In addition, the Riksdag resolved to introduce the recruitment of young conscripts, but their period of training was very short and they could purchase exemption. During the late Nineteenth Century the Riksdag debated the introduction of a new military system based on national service. The 1860's witnessed the formation of a voluntary corps of sharpshooters, who stood for a voluntary arming of the people according to the Swiss model. The movement received enthusiastic support from the public, but in time the numerous associations were transformed into a civilian league under a board of directors.

It was not until 1901 that the Riksdag passed an act providing for a new Army organization based entirely on conscription. As far as the Navy was concerned, sail was replaced by steam, and wooden vessels by steel and iron-clad designs. The iron-clads were supplemented by cruisers and torpedo boats, destroyers and submarines. In 1914 the first flying squadrons were formed.

The union with Norway proved a disappointment to the Swedes. It remained a personal union and did not lead to any closer relationship between the countries. During the late Nineteeth Century Norway underwent a marked economic expansion with a rapid growth of her Merchant Navy and a degree of industrialization which at times surpassed that of Sweden. Politically, too, Norway lay ahead of Sweden. In 1884 Norway introduced cabinet government, and fourteen years later – long before Sweden – universal franchise was granted to men throughout the country.

Throughout the entire period national feeling was growing in Norway. Simultaneously with the economic and political gains, Norway was enjoying a Golden Age of art, literature and music. All these factors formed the background for the Norwegian need for self-assertion which finally led to the dissolution of the union so that Norway could live a life of her own as an independent nation. In 1905 the union ceased to exist, following Swedish-Norwegian negotiations and after an extraordinary session of the Riksdag had approved the agreement.

Under Charles XV's brother and successor, Oscar II, Sweden began to come into closer relations with the new German Empire. Trade expanded between Sweden and Germany. Of special importance was the export of Swedish iron ore to German industry.

The dissolution of the union in 1905 resulted in a kind of national cohesion in Sweden. The Liberals looked with confidence to the future. Many technologists and business men were also optimistic. Among these was Alfred Nobel, who donated his fortune to a foundation for the awarding of annual prizes to those people who in different spheres "rendered the greatest good to humanity". The Nobel prizes, which were first awarded in 1901, made Sweden known throughout the world.

In 1910 the Swedish Army received a standard other ranks' uniform for the first time. The tricorne Carolean hat came into its own again. The Royal Army Museum.

The Triumph of Parliamentarianism

In 1865 the mediaeval Riksdag of the Estates was abolished and replaced by a bicameral Riksdag. While the First Chamber mainly represented the upper-classes, the Second was more popular in character. Politically the new Riksdag represented only 20 per cent of the adult male population. Women lacked the right to vote.

The result of the Riksdag election was a disappointment to those who had hoped that the middle-class would dominate both chambers. In the main the election meant a victory for the peasants, who joined together in the Farmers' Union, which was always in opposition to the industrialists and high officials who dominated the First Chamber.

The old antagonisms between town and country, between noblemen and peasants, were transformed at the turn of the century into antagonism between the parties of the Left and of the Right. The old Farmers Union joined the Conservatives, but in 1913 a special Agrarian Party was formed. The Liberals had a party of their own.

Meanwhile the popular movements were actively engaged in transforming society and demanding universal franchise. While the Labour Movement had a party of its own, the Social Democrats, the Revivalists and the Temperance people worked as pressure groups in the various political parties. They received much help from the radical authors – above all August Strindberg – who challenged the traditional social ideas and their institutions – Royalism, the Established Church, Militarism and Nationalism – and subjected them to debate.

The Parties agreed that a voting reform was necessary. The

This statue of August Strindberg by Carl Eldh emphasizes the obstinate and contentious traits of the writer. Photograph: Ann Grönhammar.

question was, how. In 1907 a Conservative Government under Arvid Lindman pushed through a reform. This implied the democratization of the First Chamber, while the right of voting for the Second Chamber was universal for men (although still restricted by income and capital circumstances). The voting age was to be 24. Women still lacked the vote.

As a result of the reform, which became law in 1909, those entitled to vote amounted to 19 per cent of the inhabitants of the country, as compared with the previous 9.5 per cent. The new regulations were first applied in the Election of 1911, and the result was a victory for the Liberals and the Social Democrats. Karl Staaf formed a Liberal Government and enacted several important reforms. A Labour Safety Act was passed and in 1913 an Act was passed granting Old Age Pensions to all who attained the age of 67.

The Liberals wished to cut down the costs of defence in favour of a policy of social reform, but political tension abroad convinced Staaf that national defence must gradually be strengthened. The Conservatives, on the other hand, demanded an immediate solution. The Farmers marched to Stockholm in February 1914, and in his speech to the 30,000 participants in the Palace courtyard, Gustavus V declared his support of the farmers' demands. The King's speech resulted in a constitutional crisis. The Liberal Government resigned and Hjalmar Hammarskjöld became the head of a pro-defence Conservative Government.

On the outbreak of war in 1914 Sweden declared her neutrality. It turned out to be difficult, however, to combine a strict policy of neutrality with the demands of foreign trade. Swedish trade with belligerent Germany increased considerably. Sweden imported coal in exchange for iron ore. In 1917 the Left-Wing parties won the Riksdag election. The Liberals under Nils Edén formed the Government – ever since then the parliamentary system has been upheld as a principle in Sweden. The Social Democrat Hjalmar Branting became Minister of Finance.

The war brought about severe shortages. The winter of 1917 was the severest experienced by the nation since the war years in the 1860's. Immediately after the war a virulent form of influenza caused numerous deaths. Internal differences increased. A major foreign policy issue was to increase internal controversy still further. Finland won her independence and Sweden recognized the new state. Shortly afterwards a

In July 1914 a German Albatross aircraft landed on the Ladugård heath in Stockholm. A mishap prevented it from taking off. The aircraft was copied in Sweden and 26 Albatross planes were built in Swedish factories. Later the plane was rebuilt and about 1927 it became the first instructional aircraft of the new Swedish Air Force under the designation SK 1. Maximum height: 2,500 metres, maximum speed: 120 km per hour. One aircraft of this kind is preserved at the Air Force Museum at Malmslätt.

civil war broke out, and many Swedes took part on the side of the "White" Government. In February 1918 the Swedish Government ordered a somewhat controversial naval expedition to Åland to protect the islanders from Russian "Red" forces. This operation aroused fierce criticism on the part of the Finns, who feared that the Swedes would remain on the islands. The expedition soon returned to Sweden.

In November 1918 the First World War ended. With the support of radical voices the Government was able to enact reforms bringing about Universal franchise for both men and women for elections to the Second Chamber and for local government. People were entitled to vote at the age of 23. Thanks to these reforms, 54 per cent of the population was entitled to vote. In 1919 the eight-hour day was introduced into Sweden.

The Foundation of the People's Home

Following the First World War there were large-scale social upheavals and increased movement between the classes of society. Pressure was applied from many sides, popular movements including the Cooperative Society, people's high schools, educational movements and the press. Power spread into the hands of new groupings, to white-collared employees and those engaged in the principal popular movements, to doctors, farmers, university graduates and workers.

The parties consolidated themselves throughout the country and the gap between the Right and the Left became more marked. Provincial differences were levelled, and the social structure of the various counties exercised a decisive influence. On the whole there were strong links between parties and social groups. Associations of this kind worked for remarkable stability throughout the country.

In the 1920's women achieved virtual equality with men with regard to the vote, the right to government employment and to authority in the family. In 1927 girls received the right of entry to the upper secondary schools on the same terms as boys.

In 1920 Sweden became a member of the League of Nations. Sweden's situation had improved since the war. Both Germany and Russia had been weakened. Finland had become independent and a cordon sanitaire consisting of Estonia, Latvia, Lithuania and Poland stretched along the eastern shore of the Baltic. In the circumstances both Liberals and Social Democrats considered that disarmament was possible.

In 1925 a Social Democratic Government assumed power. Hjalmar Branting, the Grand Old Man of the Labour Movement, died the same year. The Prime Minister was now Rickard Sandler with Per Albin Hansson as Minister of Defence. The same year a resolution was passed which implied a considerable reduction of the strength of the Armed Forces. Many old regiments were disbanded. The only positive factor was the establishment of a special Air Force. The decision was based on a false conception of the flexibility of the Armed Forces. It turned out that disarmament yielded poor economic results, and the rearmament which followed in the 1930's proved extremely costly and difficult to implement, due to the tense external situation.

The period 1926–1930 was a time of expansion in Sweden. Industry offered employment to a growing number of people. Mechanization and specialisation provided the solutions for the time. In the 1920's Ivar Kreuger built up an international finance group. This was based on the Swedish Match Company which, through subsidiaries abroad, controlled much of the world's production of matches.

People spoke of a second Swedish Golden Age. Unemployment was a thing of the past, the standard of living was rising for all groups. Much was spoken of recreation. In the 1920's the wireless came to Sweden. Swedish films experienced their own Golden Age. In 1927 the first Volvo was delivered in Gothenburg. Buses and lorries supplemented railway traffic. Swedes began to construct aircraft already during the war years.

In an entirely new way Swedes became conscious of the world beyond their own frontiers. The main political parties sent representatives to the League of Nations. The Social Democratic Professor Östen Unden became Sweden's principal spokeman on international law. Archbishop Nathan Söderblom invited Christians throughout the world to an ecumenical meeting in Stockholm in 1925.

In 1930 Sweden was hit by the great world crisis. The export of Sweden's three staple commodities – wood, iron ore, iron and steel – sharply declined, and companies were forced to reduce wages and dismiss workers.

The following year Sweden was shaken by the Kreuger crash. The slump had hit Kreuger's companies very hard. In March 1932 he committed suicide. The result was a panic at the Stock Exchange and shares in his companies became worthless. Many people were ruined. A board of inquiry revealed that the Group was guilty of swindling. The Riksdag guaranteed support, and Swedish industry and commerce recovered in the main.

After the Election of 1932 a Social Democratic Government under Per Albin Hansson as Prime Minister assumed office. The Social Democrats' programme envisaged large government grants to alleviate unemployment. The programme necessitated the increase of taxation. An agreement was reached between the Social Democrats and the Agrarian Party in 1933. The agreement was reached on the understanding that the Agrarian Party approved the programme for unemployment on condition that the Social Democrats approved the wishes of the Agrarian Party. There were no major economic effects, because industry had already begun to recover, but the country had now a strong Government. Cooperation between workers and farmers was to continue until the end of the 1950's.

Per Albin Hansson often spoke of "the People's Home" as the aim of the Government's efforts. Unemployment insurance was introduced in 1934. Building and construction work started. City dwellers moved in large numbers to the suburbs in the immediate vicinity of Nature. To stimulate the forming of families and to increase the birth-rate the Riksdag passed resolutions granting state housing loans and grants to mothers.

In 1938 the Employers' Confederation and the Federation of Trades Unions agreed on the rationalization of negotiation procedures and rules for the pensioning and dismissal of employees. The same year an act was passed guaranteeing an annual 12-day holiday. Books and magazines abroad described Sweden as "the Land of the Middle Way", a model country for relations between employers and wage-earners.

*In the 1930's the Social Democrats preached a People's Home ideology which seemed attractive to large groups other than manual labourers. Thanks to this wide appeal, the Social Democrats achieved a majority in the Second Chamber in 1936. Photograph: Archives of the Labour Movement.*P

The Second World War

Like most small countries Sweden had placed her faith in the League of Nations. Scarcely any event in the years between the wars aroused such indignation in Sweden as Fascist Italy's attack on Abyssinia, a country with which Sweden had had good relations over a long period. The sanctions imposed by the League of Nations were ineffectual. After international diplomatic efforts failed to establish international order, Sweden had to look to her own defences. The resolution on this subject was passed in 1936, but there was still a shortage of effective weapons.

At the end of the 1930's the four neutral Scandinavian countries stood politically close to one another. Ministers from all four countries held regular meetings. A proposal for military cooperation between Sweden and Finland was quashed due to Russian objections.

When the war broke out in 1939, Sweden declared her neutrality. The first strain on this policy was felt in connection with the Russian attack on Finland in November 1939. A strong movement adopted the slogan "The Cause of Finland is Our Cause". Thousands of volunteers offered their services and set off for the front, arms and money were collected for the sister nation, but the Government refused to intervene. The Government also turned down the offer of the Western Powers to send troops through Sweden to Finland.

The next crisis was the German occupation of Denmark and Norway on 9th April 1940. While the war was still being fought in Norway, the Germans demanded transit for their forces and arms through Sweden to Narvik, which was under siege. The Government granted this request, but not until

The Swedish Tiger was used in the Second World War as a psychological symbol to warn people against passing on secrets to strange persons. The phrase ***en svensk tiger*** *carries a double meaning – not only "A Swedish Tiger" but also "A Swede remains silent" or in the idiom of the time "A Swede keeps mum".*

fighting in Northern Norway had ceased. Before the German attack on Russia at midsummer in 1941 the Germans requested the transit of troops from Norway to Finland. Sweden agreed on condition that the concession would not be repeated.

"Our state of preparedness is good", declared Per Albin Hansson in a radio talk immediately before war broke out. These words were intended to deceive. Economic preparedness functioned fairly well. This did not, however, apply to military preparedness. Most conscripts had received no winter training. Anti-aircraft defence was inadequate, tanks were few and small, and mechanization was undeveloped.

Large-scale military rearmament began after the outbreak

of war. In April 1940 more than 300,000 men were mobilized. After training they were stationed ready for action along the coasts and the land frontiers. The aircraft industry expanded: in June there were 800 aircraft organized in 14 wings. During this period a large number of destroyers, minesweepers and submarines were launched. Civil defence was organized, and the will to defend local areas was canalized in a new organization, the Home Guard.

In spite of strict rationing the population managed, and food supplies functioned better than had been the case in the previous war. Sweden was cut off from the west, but convoys from Gothenburg procured the necessary foodstuffs. Large-scale exports of iron ore to Germany continued. There was a certain amount of censorship of the press, but the newspapers continued to assert their rights to criticize, and in the Riksdag there was an opposition. In the autumn of 1943 the transit of German troops and arms from Norway via Sweden to Germany ceased.

During the war Sweden took care of large numbers of refugees from Norway and Denmark. When the persecution of the Jews started in Denmark, many thousands of Jews could try to cross the Sound and find asylum in Sweden. Count Folke Bernadotte's operation to rescue the victims of the concentration camps attracted much attention. The greatest rescue operation during the Second World War was carried out by the Swedish diplomat Raoul Wallenberg in Budapest. He succeeded in saving thousands of Jews before he himself was removed to an unknown fate by the Russians.

During the autumn of 1944 Sweden received a large number of refugees from Estonia, Latvia and Lithuania, from the Baltic lands now reoccupied by the Russians. In all they amounted to 35,000 people. A departure from traditional Swedish policy was the Government's decision in May 1945 to repatriate 168 Balts, who had fled to Sweden in uniform and were therefore reckoned as belligerents, although many of them had been forcibly mobilized by the Germans. The repatriation of these men aroused strong feeling in Sweden.

The Welfare State

During the war Sweden had a Coalition Government, but the motivation for this ceased after the war ended. In the summer of 1945 a Social Democratic Government took office with Per Albin Hansson as Prime Minister. When Hansson died the following year he was succeeded by Tage Erlander.

Full employment was an important goal in the Social Democratic postwar programme; other aims were industrial democracy and increased power of the state in economic affairs. The social policy of the 1930's had been concerned with improved pensions as well as security in the event of illness and accidents. The post-war Government was dedicated to a more radical policy. This affected virtually all the social care institutions themselves and resulted in a new social philosophy.

The old poorhouses disappeared, their place being taken by homes for old people, housing for pensioners and social domestic help. Children's allowances were introduced in 1947, and the municipalities built day homes for children whose parents were fully employed. During the 1950's a large number of hospitals were built or reconstructed, large wards being replaced by smaller rooms. The older hospitals were divided into casualty hospitals and long-term therapy hospitals for the elderly.

The prisons were reformed. Instead of punishment in cells there was open correctional treatment and social readjustment. Reformatories were replaced by youth community centres.

In 1950 the parties agreed to establish a nine-year comprehensive school for children of all social classes in the

Until 1974 the Hall of the Realm in the Royal Palace in Stockholm was the scene for the impressive ceremonial opening of the Riksdag.

towns and rural areas. A secondary school system was also organized with numerous two or three year lines. There was no school leaving examination in the secondary school and the Matriculation Examination was abolished in 1968. Behind the school reforms lay a demand for equality: everyone should have the same entitlement to education. Free meals at school were introduced in the 1950's.

The higher educational system was also extended. Sweden now had six universities. To the Universities of Uppsala and Lund were now added those of Stockholm, Gothenburg, Umeå and Linköping. The number of students increased rapidly and a system of student grants was introduced.

Hitherto the reforms had been resolved with a high degree of political agreement. The first major political controversy arose with respect to the national supplementary pensions scheme. The Social Democrats proposed that the scheme should be paid for by contributions from the employers and that the pensions should have a stabilized value. In the Riksdag Election of 1959 the Social Democrats' pensions plan triumphed.

The 1960's witnessed major local government reforms. 2,300 rural district councils merged into 300 large municipal bodies which acquired an up-to-date administration. Many rural areas were absorbed into the nearest town. The historical term town disappeared as an administrative concept.

In 1969 Tage Erlander resigned as Head of the Government and was succeeded by Olof Palme. Two years later the bicameral Riksdag was replaced by a Riksdag with a single chamber. In 1973 Gustavus VI Adolphus died after a reign of 23 years. He was succeeded by his grandson Charles XVI Adolphus. In connection with his accession a new constitution, the result of nearly twenty years' labour and of compromises, was adopted. Under the new constitution the King is Head of State but is deprived of all political power. The Speaker appoints those who shall form governments and the Riksdag alone possesses legislative powers.

The balance of power between the two blocs – the Social Democrats and the non-socialist parties – has for the most part been so even that both sides have preferred broad, bipartisan agreements to confrontation. The Social-Democratic Government lost the parliamentary elections of 1976 and was succeeded by a non-socialist coalition, with Center Party leader, Thorbjörn Fälldin Prime Minister. The Social-Democrats were returned to power in the elections of 1982. In February of 1986, an unknown assassin shot Prime Minister Olof Palme on a Stockholm sidewalk. Palme was succeeded by Ingvar Carlsson. The 1991 elections put the Social-Democrats out of office and brought a new non-socialist coalition to power under the leadership of the Conservative Party leader, Carl Bildt.

Sweden in the World

In 1946 Sweden joined the United Nations. Sweden also became a member of the Council of Europe and of OECC. The major parties were in agreement that Sweden should continue to pursue a policy of neutrality and not align herself with a Great Power bloc.

During the Cold War between the Soviet Union and the Western Powers following the end of the war the question of Scandinavian defence became an important issue. In the spring of 1948 Finland entered into a pact of friendship with the Soviet Union. At the same time the foreign ministries of the other three Nordic States began to consider the idea of a common Nordic defence. The following year all three governments met at Karlstad, but the negotiations broke down. Norway and Denmark joined NATO, while Sweden alone kept firmly to her non-alliance policy.

Cooperation between the Nordic Countries continued. The Nordic Council was founded in 1953. Sweden, Norway and Denmark joined a large European free-trade association, EFTA, but this broke up in 1953 when Denmark applied to join EEC. Sweden declined membership on the grounds that it was incompatible with the policy of neutrality. On the other hand Sweden entered into a trade agreement with the European Community.

The Swedish policy of neutrality assumes a strong defence. Political agreement between the parties has also ensured that defence is maintained at a qualitatively high level.

For a number of years Swedish civil and military personnel have participated in a great many United Nations peacekeeping operations. Sweden has mainly been engaged in

The Swedish Royal Family visiting the first Stockholm Water Festival in August 1991. From the left: Prince Charles Philip, Princess Madeleine, Crown Princess Victoria, King Charles XVI Gustavus and Queen Silvia. Photo by Jan-Erik Henriksson, Svenskt Pressfoto.

humanitarian and social tasks. Since the 1970's 1 per cent of the national income has been devoted to the aid of a number of developing countries. A special government agency, SIDA, is responsible for the organization and distribution of aid to developing countries.

The world has come closer to Sweden by means of the foreign correspondents of the press, through the radio, and television, which had its break-through in Sweden in the 1950's, and through sports which contributed to the opening of Sweden's borders. Motoring and flying provided many people with a way out into the world. SAS (Scandinavian Airlines System) was founded in 1946 and ten years later a special company, Linjeflyg, was established for domestic traffic. Charter flights have enabled many Swedes to visit other countries.

In Sweden, as in many other lands, the economic and social advances have been essentially supported by the enormous expansion of industry. To an increasing extent Swedish industry has established itself abroad. The vital question is whether industry can retain its position on the foreign markets. The answer to this is what will finally determine Sweden's capacity to maintain the welfare state and give assistance to the developing countries.

Our natural environment and the many threats to plant and animal species, to the atmosphere and water that industrial society poses have been a major concern in recent years. The National Swedish Environment Protection Board was established in 1967. Sweden has been a forerunner when it comes to conservation, but much remains to be done. The Swedish people wholeheartedly accept the prosperity industrialism has produced and the far-reaching transformation of Swedish society, yet they still have strong ties to the countryside.

The social upheaval in Eastern Europe and the fall of communism there have eroded the traditional rationale for the Swedish policy of non-alignment and neutrality. In the autumn of 1990, the four largest parliamentary parties gave the Social-Democratic Government a mandate to open negotiations concerning Swedish membership in the European Community. The negotiations are currently in progress.